## At Issue

# I The Occupy Movement

# Other Books in the At Issue Series:

# At Issue

# ▎The Occupy Movement

*Stefan Kiesbye*

**GREENHAVEN PRESS**
*A part of Gale, Cengage Learning*

GALE
CENGAGE Learning·

Detroit • New York • San Francisco • New Haven, Conn • Waterville, Maine • London

Elizabeth Des Chenes, *Director, Publishing Solutions*

© 2013 Greenhaven Press, a part of Gale, Cengage Learning

Gale and Greenhaven Press are registered trademarks used herein under license.

*For more information, contact:*
Greenhaven Press
27500 Drake Rd.
Farmington Hills, MI 48331-3535
Or you can visit our Internet site at gale.cengage.com

For product information and technology assistance, contact us at

Gale Customer Support, 1-800-877-4253
For permission to use material from this text or product, submit all requests online at www.cengage.com/permissions

Further permissions questions can be emailed to permissionrequest@cengage.com

Articles in Greenhaven Press anthologies are often edited for length to meet page requirements. In addition, original titles of these works are changed to clearly present the main thesis and to explicitly indicate the author's opinion. Every effort is made to ensure that Greenhaven Press accurately reflects the original intent of the authors. Every effort has been made to trace the owners of copyrighted material.

Cover image copyright © Images.com/Corbis.

LIBRARY OF CONGRESS CATALOGING-IN-PUBLICATION DATA

The occupy movement / Stefan Kiesbye, book editor.
    p. cm. -- (At issue)
Includes bibliographical references and index.
    ISBN 978-0-7377-6486-4 (hardcover) -- ISBN 978-0-7377-6487-1 (pbk.)
1. Occupy movement. 2. Income distribution--United States--Public opinion. 3. Equality--United States--Public opinion. 4. Protest movements--United States--History--21st century. 5. Public opinion--United States. I. Kiesbye, Stefan.
    HC110.I5O26 2012
    339.20973--dc23

                                                                    2012030376

Printed in the United States of America
1 2 3 4 5        16 15 14 13 12

# Contents

# Introduction

In his January 8, 2012 article for *Salon.com*, "What Occupy Can Learn from the *Hunger Games*," critic Mike Doherty writes that while there is "no necessary cause-and-effect relationship between world events and publishing phenomena . . . there can certainly be a resonance." Doherty notes that while author Suzanne Collins states that her *Hunger Games* trilogy was inspired by the Iraq war, her books raise questions about economic inequality and greed, and government control of information, which are of even more importance.

According to Doherty, Collins's heroine, Katniss Everdeen, faces problems that have many parallels to the issues that concern the Occupy Movement, lending her story—and similar Young Adult novels—a new urgency. Both Katniss and the Occupy Movement are concerned about societies that are sharply divided and where conflicting ideologies threaten to defeat reform and change.

Doherty points out that although Katniss and fellow heroes and heroines must survive in the wilderness,

> they're self-aware [and in] the wild, they find misfits who safeguard learning, hoarding the books and lore that the dystopias have repressed. The Occupy movement often casts itself in a similar light, as its members "rough it" in parks in the middle of cities as if keeping alive a more earthy, simple, honest way of living; their library tents symbolize their devotion to learning from the past as they forge a better way for the future. Indeed, the library is a synecdoche for the movement itself: in Toronto, protesters chained themselves to theirs as it was about to be removed as part of the camp's eviction; at Occupy Wall Street, the demolishing of the library has been viewed as a repressive dystopian act.

Unlike other literary heroes who could count on the audience's sympathy and goodwill because their lives on the page or screen are beyond reproach, Katniss or author Patrick Ness's Viola from *Chaos Walking*, are themselves dangerous, and can easily turn on people who were once allies. Far from obeying the rebel leader Alma Coin, Katniss chooses to kill her, because Coin, just like the leaders of the previous regime, is corrupted by power and wealth. Instead of following a current ideology or its direct opposite, this new breed of heroes tries for a third way, opting to seek alliances between small, independent groups and eschewing grand ideological schemes.

As Doherty explains,

[i]n "*The Hunger Games*," Katniss ultimately undermines the regimes of both President Snow and Alma Coin, throwing her society into disarray but perhaps helping to usher in what one character calls "the evolution of the human race" . . . Stories of people who are trampled on by competing ideologies and broken by enforced scarcity are certainly apt at a time when the U.S. political system is regularly brought to a standstill by politicians unwaveringly devoted to ideologies, the European Union threatens to disintegrate due to its members' conflicting demands, divisions between the rich and the poor are ever-increasing, and those with the power to help offer rhetoric instead. The Occupy movement, as a loosely affiliated band of concerned people—Marxists, anarchists, environmentalists, survivalists, and more—has on the whole avoided ideology and embraced diversity and democracy.

Doherty's sentiment is echoed in an April 23, 2012, article, "Evening the Odds," by *New Yorker* contributor Nicholas Lemann. Writing about the current political debate, which is becoming increasingly polarizing, he states that "if we are to go further—and get the political system to try seriously to reverse the trends of the past thirty years [the inequality of income and wealth]—somebody will have to figure out how to stitch together a coalition of distinct, smaller interest groups that, in their different ways, care deeply about inequality, and, together, can pressure Washington in favor of specific policies."

To be sure, neither the *Hunger Games* nor other Young Adult novels offer easy solutions to how this coalition can be forged, or how dystopian regimes can be replaced by more peaceful and democratic alternatives. And yet, in life and in art, we might approach a point in which a movement such as Occupy Wall Street (and its many offshoots) can influence the political debate and exact change. Whether the current movement can succeed or whether it is bound to disband and fail will be discussed in *At Issue: The Occupy Movement*. Supporters, critics, and political observers discuss the impact of the Occupy Movement as well as its future and possible evolution into a larger political force.

# 1

# The Occupy Movement Is a Patriotic Protest Against Greed and Corruption

*Norman Lear*

*Norman Lear is a television writer and producer who produced such sitcoms as* All in the Family, Sanford and Son, One Day at a Time, *and* The Jeffersons. *He also founded the civil liberties advocacy organization People for the American Way in 1981 and has supported First Amendment rights and liberal causes.*

*At a time when many Americans are suffering from the consequences of the economic downturn, political groups try to blame underrepresented groups and use public anger and frustration for their own betterment. The Occupy Movement is a sign that people are fed up with demagogues and are taking a deeply patriotic stand against special interests and the ever-widening gap between the very rich and those who are left out of the American Dream.*

I was recently shown a picture from one of the Occupy protests taking place across the country. It featured a young woman surrounded by police. She was the only protester in the picture, but she didn't seem intimidated. All by herself, up against the police barricade, she held a handwritten sign saying simply "I am a born again American."

I've never met this woman, but I think I know exactly what she's feeling.

## An Awakening

I had my first "born again American" moment 30 years ago, when I was moved to outrage and action by a group of hate-preaching televangelists who were trying to claim sole ownership of patriotism, faith and flag for the far right. One of them asked his viewing congregation to pray for the removal of a Supreme Court justice.

I did what I knew how to do and produced a 60-second TV spot. It featured a factory worker whose family members, all Christians, held an array of political beliefs. He didn't believe that anyone, not even a minister, had a right to judge whether people were good or bad Christians based on their political views. "That's not the American way," he wound up saying. I ran it on local TV, and it was picked up by the networks. People For the American Way [Civil Liberties Advocacy Group] grew out of the overwhelming response to that ad.

One of the most encouraging things to happen in 2011 was the birth of the Occupy Wall Street movement, which is giving the entire country the chance for a "born again American" moment. In calling attention to the country's widening chasm between rich and poor, the Occupiers have unleashed decades of pent-up patriotic outrage against the systematic violation of our nation's core principles by the "say good-bye to the middle class" alliance of the neocons, theocons and corporate America.

## Taking Action

To those many millions of Americans whose guts tell them the Occupy movement is on to something, but aren't the sort to camp out or protest in the street, I say find another way to let your voice be heard in the new year. Work with others who share your passion for equal opportunity and equal justice for all Americans, and find ways to channel outrage into productive action. I'm betting you'll find, as I have over my nearly four score plus 10, that you'll form some of the most rewarding relationships and have some of the most meaningful experiences of your life.

I have been lucky in many ways. I was raised by my immigrant grandfather to treasure the freedom and opportunities America offers. I also learned early to fear the power of demagogues with megaphones, as an 11-year-old listening to the anti-Semitic ravings and attacks on President Franklin D. Roosevelt from radio priest Father [Charles] Coughlin, the spiritual godfather of those who poison our airwaves and online forums today. By the time I was a teenager, I knew that the values of individual and religious liberty were worth fighting for, which is why I dropped out of college to enlist in the war against [Adolf] Hitler.

---

*Work with others who share your passion for equal opportunity and equal justice for all Americans, and find ways to channel outrage into productive action.*

---

Since then I have repeatedly seen Americans get off their couches to hold this country accountable to its stated values. They did it to fight for civil rights and the dismantling of the legal apartheid of Jim Crow; for the women's movement; for equality for lesbian, gay, bisexual and transgender Americans. They have rallied to ensure that immigrants are treated with dignity and justice. All these efforts to overcome bigotry and institutionalized prejudice are still works in progress, but I am awed by the progress we have made.

Generations of Americans have worked to create a nation in which individual liberty can thrive alongside commitment to the principle that all members of a community should have the opportunity to pursue their dreams and build a decent life for themselves and their families. In recent decades, that dream has been betrayed.

---

*Many Americans are in despair, and it has left them open to demagoguery and political manipulation.*

---

## Working to Curb Greed and Corruption

The religious right leaders who got me engaged in politics often portray such things as free expression and equal protection for all Americans no matter their race, religion or sexual orientation as anti-Christian and un-American, as symptoms of cultural decline. I couldn't disagree more. What strikes me as un-American are the greed, deception and systematic corruption that have infected politics, business and so much of our culture in recent years. Some of those with power and privilege have worked to create a system that continually reinforces that privilege and power, leaving ever-increasing numbers of Americans without reasonable hope for the kind of life their parents worked to give them.

Many Americans are in despair, and it has left them open to demagoguery and political manipulation. Blame gays, liberals, unions, immigrants or feminists for your family's struggles, for shrinking economic opportunity, for foreclosures and disappearing wages and benefits. Blame secularists or Muslims, or both, for the sense that our values have gone haywire.

A year out from the 2012 election, I am already tired of those who use the phrase "American exceptionalism" to reassert the far-right's claim that God, the Founding Fathers and any decent freedom-loving American must share their reactionary political agenda. I embrace the idea too that our nation should be a "shining city on a hill." We are the spiritual heirs to those Americans who struggled to end slavery and segregation, to end child labor and win safe conditions and living wages for workers, to enable every American to enrich his or her community and country by finding a place and a way to flourish in the world. We must make ourselves worthy of that legacy.

## Protest Is a Patriotic Calling

Call it the American dream, the American promise or the American way. Whatever term you use, it is imperiled, and worth fighting for. It is that basic, deeply patriotic emotion that I believe is finding expression—bottom-up, small-d democratic expression—in the Occupy movement. We can, and I would say must, fully embrace both love of country and outrage at attempts to despoil it. What better cause? What better time?

# 2

# The Occupy Movement Is Based on Resentment and Misinterpretations

*Steve Chapman*

*Steve Chapman is a columnist and editorial writer for the* Chicago Tribune. *His twice-a-week column on national and international affairs appears in many newspapers across the country, and he has written articles for* Slate, The American Spectator, National Review, *and* The Weekly Standard.

*The Occupy protesters are acting on false assumptions, blaming rich entrepreneurs and corporations for a perceived gap between the very wealthy and middle-class America. However, wealth is not a limited resource and has increased in decades past. Furthermore, the financial elite's success has not come at the expense of Main Street America, but has contributed to overall wealth.*

If you want to know what motivates the people involved in Occupy Wall Street [OWS], you can get a good idea from *Think Progress*, a left-leaning website. It offers a map of the continental United States labeled, "If U.S. land were divided like U.S. wealth."

In this representation, 1 percent of the people hold title to most of the West and Great Plains area. Nine percent have a swath about the same size stretching from Minnesota south to

Oklahoma and east to Maine. The other 90 percent of the population get only a narrow slice along the southern rim.

It's a stark, dramatic representation of the problem as OWS sees it. It's also a perfect illustration of the movement's economic misunderstandings.

Land, after all, is more or less fixed in supply. I can't obtain more of it unless someone gives up theirs. If the top 10 percent owned most of the land and barred everyone else from it, the rest would be pretty squeezed.

## Wealth Has No Natural Limits

But wealth and income are not like land. To start with, they are not limited in supply—they can multiply many times over without end, and they have done just that. And, unlike with patches of soil, everyone can get more without anyone consigned to less.

There is not much more land in America than there was 50 years ago. But there is far more wealth. Since 1960, the total output of the U.S. economy, accounting for inflation, has more than quadrupled. Total physical assets have done likewise.

The conviction among OWS activists is that the rich have improved their lot by taking money from the not so rich— that wealth has been cruelly redistributed upward. What they overlook is that the real gains come from the creation of new wealth.

---

*There is not much more land in America than there was 50 years ago. But there is far more wealth.*

---

Steve Jobs [co-founder and former CEO of Apple Inc.] did exceptionally well for himself, but he made the broad mass of consumers, here and abroad, better off in the process. Same for Sam Walton [founder of Walmart and Sam's Club]. What

Oprah Winfrey created made her rich, but without her, those creations wouldn't have existed to entertain and gratify her audience.

Ten years ago, the richest person on Earth couldn't buy a device that does what the iPhone does. Today, anyone can get one free upon signing a two-year carrier contract. Entry-level cars are vastly better in amenities and reliability than your father's Cadillac decades ago.

---

*The wealthy are far better off than they used to be. But their improvement has not come at the expense of those down the economic ladder.*

---

## The Standard of Living Has Improved

Lifesaving and life-changing medicines and therapies once unknown are now commonplace. Food costs a fraction of what it once did. TV viewers used to have three channels to choose from. Now they have hundreds.

The wealthy are far better off than they used to be. But their improvement has not come at the expense of those down the economic ladder. Economists Bruce D. Meyer of the University of Chicago and James X. Sullivan of the University of Notre Dame find that over the past three decades, both the poor and the middle class have made substantial material progress.

"Median income and consumption both rose by more than 50 percent in real terms between 1980 and 2009," they reported last month [October 2011] in a paper for the conservative American Enterprise Institute in Washington [DC]. Those in the bottom tenth of the income ladder enjoyed comparable gains.

Not that everything is copacetic [in excellent order]. The Great Recession has wrought havoc on the middle class and the poor—eliminating jobs, reducing income, and slashing the value of homes.

## The Recession Has Hit Everyone

But if it's any consolation, the rich have seen their take shrink as well. Between 2007 and 2009, notes Steven Kaplan of the University of Chicago Booth School of Business, the share of all income going to the richest 1 percent of Americans fell by a full quarter.

The miserable reality today is not that the many are doing worse because our capitalist system is set up to fleece them for the benefit of the few. They are doing worse because the economy went through a cataclysm from which it has yet to recover.

When the economy crashes, it's those with the least education, fewest options, and slimmest resources who suffer most. That's true, by the way, in non-capitalist societies as well as capitalist ones. In either, people who have done nothing wrong often suffer.

At moments like this, it's not surprising that many Americans would resent the wealthy and feel the urge to punish them. But the OWS demand for action against them is the equivalent of honking your horn when you're stuck in a traffic jam. It makes a lot of noise, without getting you anywhere.

# 3

# The Occupy Movement Is Being Fueled by Government Demagoguery

*Liz Peek*

*Liz Peek worked as a research analyst on Wall Street before becoming a columnist for* The New York Sun, Women on the Web, *the* Motley Fool, *and* FoxNews.com. *She appears regularly on Fox News'* Strategy Room *and has been a guest on* Larry Kudlow, Fox and Friends, *and various Fox Business programs.*

*Instead of a predicted labor shortage, America is facing high unemployment. The Occupy Movement's stance against the widening gap between the rich and the poor is misguided at best. Corporations and investors have not worked to disenfranchise workers and employees, but have been forced to bow to international markets' pressure and eliminate jobs to compete overseas. Mechanization and outsourcing have eroded the job market, but blaming Wall Street is wrongheaded. Instead, the federal government needs to implement rewards for those willing to hire new workers and rethink tax breaks for investors. Only if the president can create an unbiased dialogue about America's financial future and bring together warring factions will the United States be able to succeed.*

In 2003, labor expert John Challenger confidently wrote of *The Coming Labor Shortage*, predicting that the graying of America's workforce would result in too few workers and cautioning that "labor shortages may become so severe that retirement as we know it will vanish."

This prediction was taken so seriously that the Congressional Research Service addressed the potential problem as recently as 2008, in a report entitled "Retiring Baby-Boomers = A Labor Shortage?" The document suggests that the low unemployment rate for 2007—4.6%—might indeed be a harbinger of "tight labor conditions that are related to long-running demographic trends."

## The Reasons of Unemployment

If only! With 14.8 million people out of work today, you wonder: how did they get it so wrong? Some of the shift from shortage to excess can certainly be explained by the recession. But the premise was wobbly from the start, especially given the damaging, and determining, confluence of events over recent decades:

- The wholesale migration of women into the workforce

- The massive automation of factory floors, farms, banks, travel businesses, and nearly every other sort of commercial undertaking

- The rising life expectancy of workers

- And, to top it off, globalization and the increased ease of exporting output overseas.

It seems so obvious.

It is also obvious that none of these trends is about to disappear. Moreover, it is clear that policy makers in the U.S. and around the world have failed to deal with the increased challenge of creating jobs. This is not just an American problem. It is an issue in the EU [European Union], where, despite an aging workforce, unemployment currently stands at 9.5% and job production is scarce. It is also a crisis in Egypt, where nearly one third of the population is under the age of 14 and unemployment is running close to 12%. It is even a problem in China, where the ongoing (though slowed) migrations from countryside to city pressure local governments to maintain "social stability" by providing work.

*The New York Times* dubiously asserted last weekend [in October 2011] that the Occupy Wall Street crowd and those protesting around the world were "united in frustration with the widening gap between the rich and the poor." (I have listened carefully to interviews with the protesters in recent weeks and have never heard expressed such a cogent grievance.) The angry demonstrators are probably not interested in a debate about the origins of that gap, but our policymakers should be. It should be at the heart of our "industrial policy," should we ever gear up to adopt one, and should also guide any overhaul of our tax policy.

---

*Money spent on mechanized call centers, assembly lines, gas pumps, and the rest reduced but did not eliminate the pressure from countries like China and India, where workers were willing to work for far less than our own.*

---

## The Dominating Role of Capital

Economic theory would argue that the rent due to the various components of production—labor and capital—varies in proportion to the availability of, and need for, those ingredients. The cause of the widening gap between rich and poor has been not some nefarious [wicked] corporate behavior but rather the increased demand for and higher rent paid to capital over the past few decades—capital that was invested in automation in part to keep our industries competitive with cheap labor abroad. Money spent on mechanized call centers, assembly lines, gas pumps, and the rest reduced but did not eliminate the pressure from countries like China and India, where workers were willing to work for far less than our own. These expenditures yielded high profits, and return on capital consequently rose.

At the same time, the availability of labor—because of more women workers, seniors who in earlier times might have retired, and foreigners now accessible through increased communications—outpaced demand. Bingo! The earnings attached to labor dropped relative to the return on capital.

This growing disparity, having never been recognized, has also not been addressed. In fact, our government has embraced one measure after another that has further driven up the cost of workers, unwittingly tilting the balance even further towards the use of capital to minimize labor. Rising minimum wages, payroll taxes (the Social Security tax for instance started out at 2% but is currently 12.4%), work rules that diminish productivity—these costs have improved prospects for those employed but dampened overall demand for workers.

---

*In fact, our government has embraced one measure after another that has further driven up the cost of workers, unwittingly tilting the balance even further towards the use of capital to minimize labor.*

---

## Using Taxes to Encourage Hiring

Those unhappy that wealthy people sometimes pay less in taxes relative to income than the middle class should blame our tax policies. A greater percentage of wealthy people's income is generated by capital gains, interest, and dividends, which are taxed at a lower rate because the government has wanted to encourage savings and investment. However, as technological change accelerated, the economic benefits of investing in labor-saving devices soared; arguably, there was no need to provide further incentives. People investing in productivity-driven profits through the stock market were handsomely rewarded.

Our society is facing great strains. Until we put people back to work, the tensions between those funding government services and those consuming them will only expand. We need to explore whether tax breaks given to investors are as important to our society going forward as policies that would reward businesses for hiring workers. Permanent elimination of payroll taxes or long-term adoption of tax credits for hiring, as opposed to temporary measures for instance, might be considered.

We are only beginning to have this conversation. Unhappily, it is wrapped up in populist politics. President [Barack] Obama has done this country enormous harm by pitting one group against another; his successful efforts to whip up fury against the producing class in this country is repugnant and wrong-headed. What is clear is that all groups will have to sign on to get our country back on track and that we need a president who can embrace novel approaches—and take the country along with him. We may not have a shortage of labor, but we are surely struggling with a shortage of leadership.

# 4

# The Occupy Movement Aims to End Capitalist Excesses

*Kevin Zeese*

*Kevin Zeese is the co-director of news website* It's Our Economy *and one of the original organizers of Occupy Washington, DC.*

*While the occupations across America have been successful in raising awareness of the nation's financial inequality, the Occupy Movement has to look for different routes to build momentum. Local organizing, media coverage, and the use of the Internet will spread the movement's message and lead to better conditions for those at the bottom of the economic ladder. Occupying parks and streets was only a first step; now the protesters need to use their energy and resources to organize a movement that can equal the Civil Rights and Women's Suffrage movements.*

With encampments being closed across the country it is important to remember the end goal is not to occupy public space, it is to end corporate rule. We seek to replace the rule of money with the rule of people. Occupying is a tactic but the grand strategy of the Occupy Movement is to weaken the pillars that hold the corporate-government in place by educating, organizing and mobilizing people into an independent political force.

## The Wealth Divide

The occupations of public space have already done a great deal to lift the veil of lies. People are now more aware than ever that the wealth divide is caused by a rigged economic system of crony capitalism and that we can create a fair economy that works for all Americans. We are also aware that many of our fellow citizens are ready to take action—extreme action of sleeping outside in the cold in a public park. And, we also now know that we have the power to shift the debate and force the economic and political elites to listen to us. In just a few months [especially at the end of 2011] we have made a difference.

Occupying public space involves a lot of resources and energy that could be spent educating, organizing and mobilizing people in much greater numbers. There is a lot to do to end corporate rule and the challenges of occupying public space can divert our attention and resources from other responsibilities we have as a movement.

When we were organizing the Occupation of Washington, DC—before the occupation of Wall Street began—we were in conversation with movements around the world. The Spanish Indignados [Protesters for Financial and Social Reforms] told us that an occupation should last no more than two weeks. After that it becomes a diversion from the political objectives. The occupation begins to spend its time dealing with poverty, homelessness, inadequately treated mental illness and addiction—this has been experienced by occupiers across the country.

## Timing Occupations Successfully

Occupying for a short time accomplishes many of the objectives of holding public space—the political dialogue is affected, people are mobilized and all see that fellow citizens can effectively challenge the corporate-state. Staying for a lengthy period continues to deepen these goals but the impacts are more limited and the costs get higher.

What to do next? The Occupy Movement needs to bring participatory democracy to communities. Occupiers should develop an aggressive organizing plan for their city. Divide the city and appoint people to be responsible for different areas of the city. Depending on how many people you have make these areas as small as possible. Develop plans for house-to-house campaigns where you knock on doors, provide literature, ask what you can do to make their lives better. Do they need snow removed? Clothes? If so, get the occupy team to fulfill their needs, find used clothes, clean their yard—whatever you can do to help. This shows community and builds relationships.

Plan a march through the different communities in the city. Make it a spectacle. Have a marching band. Don't have one—reach out to local school bands. Organize them. Create floats, images and signs. Display yourselves and your message. Hand out literature as you march. Let people know what the occupy stands for. They should join us in building a better world for them and their families.

---

*The Occupy Movement needs to bring participatory democracy to communities. Occupiers should develop an aggressive organizing plan for their city.*

---

Plan public General Assemblies in communities across the city. Teach people the General Assembly process, the hand signals, how to stack speakers, how to listen and reach consensus. Learn the local issues. Solve local problems. Again, build a community that works together to solve problems.

## Organizing the Movement

Let people know about the National Occupation of Washington DC (NOW DC), the American Spring beginning on March 30th [2011]. Organize people to come, share rides, hire buses, walk, ride a bike—get people to the nation's capital to show the united force of the people against the rule of money. This will be an opportunity to display our solidarity and demand that the people, not money, rule.

How rapidly a movement makes progress is hard to predict. It is never a constant upswing of growth and progress. We may be in for a sprint, or more likely, a marathon with hurdles. If you are hoping for a sprint, note that the deep corruption of the government and the economy has left both weaker than is publicly acknowledged. It may be a hollowed out shell ready to fall.

But, this may also take years to accomplish. Take the timeline of the Civil Rights movement: 1955 Rosa Parks sits in the front of the bus, not until five years later in 1960, do the lunch counter sit-ins begin. Not until three years later in 1963 does Dr. Martin Luther King, Jr. lead a march on Washington for the "I have a Dream" speech. No doubt the time between Rosa Parks and the lunch counter sit-ins and Civil Rights Act passing in 1964 seemed slow to those involved. Looking back it was rapid, transformational change. In fact, the movement grew in fits and starts and had roots decades of activity before the 1950s. In those times of seeming lull, work was being done, to educate and organize people that led to the big spurts of progress.

---

*How rapidly a movement makes progress is hard to predict. It is never a constant upswing of growth and progress.*

---

## Patience Is of the Essence

Older movements, when communication was slower, have taken even longer. The women's suffrage movement held its first convention in 1848 in Seneca Falls, NY. Twenty years later, Susan B. Anthony and Elizabeth Cady Stanton formed the National Woman Suffrage Association. In 1913, Alice Paul and Lucy Burns formed the National Women's Party to work for a constitutional amendment to give women the vote. Finally, in 1919 the federal woman's suffrage amendment, originally written by Susan B. Anthony and introduced in Congress in 1878, was passed by the House of Representatives and the Senate, sent to the states for ratification and signed into law one year later.

With mass media, and especially the new democratized media of social networks, the Internet, anonymous leaks and independent media, it is very likely the end of the rule of money will come more quickly. If we focus on our goal, act with intention and use our energy and resources wisely victory will come sooner.

---

*The elites are foolish to think they will stop this movement by closing occupations.*

---

Our challenge to corporate power has roots. The Project on Corporations Law and Democracy was founded in 1995. In 1999 the protests against the World Trade Organization occurred in Seattle. In 2000, long-time crusader against corporate power, Ralph Nader, ran his first full presidential campaign and continues to challenge corporatism. This decade has been called the "Great Turning," which Joanna Macy has defined as "the shift from the Industrial Growth Society to a life-sustaining civilization." *America Beyond Capitalism* by Gar Alperovitz, just printed its second edition, five years after the first, documenting the evolution of the developing democratized economy. These are some of the foundations on which the Occupy Movement is building as the unfairness and insecurity of corporate capitalism becomes evident to all. Our roots are deeper than the few months of our existence.

## The Evolution of Occupy Protests

The elites are foolish to think they will stop this movement by closing occupations. The Occupy Movement will evolve in new and unpredictable ways that will make the elites wish for the days of mere public encampments. The 1% should know they will be held accountable. The people have found their voice and will not be silenced. The era of the rule of money is nearing its end.

# 5

# The Occupy Movement Is Made Possible by Capitalism

*Andrew Rinehart*

*Andrew Rinehart is an entrepreneur and has been involved in local and national politics, assisting in fundraising efforts for various candidates, Mitt Romney, John McCain, George W. Bush, and Hillary and Bill Clinton. He blogs at andrewrinehart.us.*

*The Occupy Movement has raised awareness of America's financial troubles, but its efforts are misguided and largely wasted. Instead of blaming entrepreneurs for their hard-earned success, protesters should start their own businesses and become active in their communities. The occupiers can't change greed, but they can set an example and work hard to lift everyone above their current status.*

I always appreciate when people are passionate. About anything, really. Apathy is rampant today and going after something you believe in is admirable.

That doesn't mean you're right, however.

The latest social and political movement, the Occupy Wall Street Protest, is disorganized, poorly planned and horribly executed. But that's not even close to the worst part. Their mentality is extremely dangerous to just about everything that makes America great.

## The Start of a Movement

I'd heard about the protest in the last few weeks [October–November 2011]. In fact, they currently occupy a park in downtown Salt Lake City and I've seen them marching. But before I could develop a real opinion of their ideas, I simply had to see the heart of the movement in New York myself.

The New York Occupy Wall Street movement started in lower Manhattan in early August [2011] with just a dozen or so people. At the first meeting, everyone was free to talk and a facilitator moderated the discussion. The template for the protest quickly became one where everyone would be heard. What is puzzling to outsiders and maddening to the police however is that no leaders have developed. When dealing with issues of the law or sanitation, there is no point man, no one person making decisions for the group. This has made it tough to control a sometimes "rebellious" group. When the NYPD [New York Police Department] distributed fliers to notify the protesters of new rules banning sleeping bags and tents, the protesters folded the fliers into origami.

## Image Problems of the Protest

The protesters occupy a surprisingly small park in the financial district of Manhattan just around the corner from the Freedom Tower. The park is surrounded by dozens of police officers keeping an extremely watchful eye over the protest. They live in tents and sleeping bags and frankly, the majority of the protesters appear to be homeless, simply having relocated to the park from another location in the city. Dozens verified this.

Because of the free food, sleeping bags and coats in the park, the movement has a "serious problem with hangers-on" said Patrick Brumer, 23, a protester in the area.

A few fights have broken out, including one involving Tonye Iketubosin, a 26 year old man from Brooklyn, whom police charged with sexually abusing an 18 year-old woman in a tent there. On Thursday [November 3, 2011], police arrested a Florida man for punching a protester in the eye. There have been several arrests made because of the open drug use taking place. All in all however, the law breakers appear to constitute a small fringe of the group.

---

*Many of the protesters claim that they are entrepreneurs . . . but it couldn't be further from the truth.*

---

## The Goals of the Movement

So what are they protesting? As it turns out, that question is not as easily answered as one may think.

I stopped by the park to find out for myself.

When asking the protesters what it is that they are protesting, an array of answers come in but all with the underlying issues being lack of jobs, corporate greed and those "crooks" on Wall Street. AKA the 1%.

I came away from my visit concerned. In fact, for the last 3 years I've been extremely concerned about the future welfare of our country but this trip only reinforced those concerns.

There is a movement taking place that is much deeper and more serious than 300 people sleeping in a park and marching the streets. It's what the growing movement actually represents and reflects on a greater scale around the world; entitlement.

I can't help but think what these thousands of people around the world could have accomplished in the last 60 days in place of participating in this protest. Imagine what they could have done in a small business of their own (nowadays, you can start a business for as little as $100), as an employee, volunteer, wife, husband, father or mother. Many of the protesters claim that they are entrepreneurs (in the same sentence, they'll ask you if you have any spare change) but it couldn't be further from the truth.

Entrepreneurs are focused on results, not handouts. Entrepreneurs work hard and know that if they can't rely on themselves to produce a paycheck, they certainly can't rely on someone else (boss). Entrepreneurs focus on tasks that increase revenue and profit and that benefit the community around them simultaneously. Entrepreneurs do not defecate in buckets, on the street or "across the road at McDonalds because that corporation is corrupt and I want to send a message" as one protester put it.

---

*I can't help but think what these thousands of people around the world could have accomplished in the last 60 days in place of participating in this protest.*

---

## Believing in Our Future

Finally, entrepreneurs believe in our future, our country and capitalism. They know it's what made and makes America so great and without it, the very right to protest would not exist. Without capitalism, there wouldn't be any jobs. There wouldn't be a New York City. There wouldn't be a park to sleep in and there wouldn't exist a hope for a better future.

I'm concerned when I hear that the 1% "got lucky" and that's how they became wealthy. I'm concerned when I hear that there are a growing number of Americans that want 50% plus in mandatory income tax, in order to "redistribute" the money on down. I'm concerned when I see people wanting more out of their lives but are unwilling to work to get it.

## Earning a Share of America's Wealth

You see, I don't believe that the "pie" of wealth is only so big and you had "better be given your fair share." The pie can and will grow and so will everyone's opportunity to get a bigger piece. Those willing to work hard can make their "piece" as big as they want it to be.

That's what's so great and unique about this country.

My suggestions to the protesters:

*Start a business of your own.* You can do it cheaply and easily with the internet. It will take less thought than the cardboard sign you made and require less of your time than the protest. Are you truly interested in putting those "corporate pigs" out of business? Start a competing business and do things according to the way you believe they should have been done in the first place. If you're right, the market will reward you.

*Get a job.* There are 20 million plus of them available right now. Quit holding out for that "management" position and get to work, even at minimum wage. Prove to your employer than you can work hard and get results. You will be compensated based on the value you deliver.

*Have a problem with something in America? Your voice can be heard virtually anywhere and you are free to protest.* But narrow your focus in on the actual problem and problem creators. Protesting "greed" is similar to protesting bad weather. You aren't going to change it. Get focused and gauge the results of your actions frequently.

# 6

# The Occupy Movement Is the Beginning of an Internet-Age Revolution

## Beyondborders

*Beyondborders writes that, "[I am] a world citizen, poet and advocate for citizen power and free speech. I am a PhD candidate in liberation psychology, currently working on my dissertation while connecting with our common ground of humanity as a blogger at* A World Beyond Borders.*"*

*While the Occupy protests have ties to the Civil Rights and Women's Suffrage movements, the emergence of WikiLeaks has elevated the occupations to a new globalized level. Since WikiLeaks exposes fraud and abuse around the world, protests in the Middle East and elsewhere have been able to spread and influence people worldwide. Instead of waiting for politicians to reform the political and financial systems, protesters have taken action themselves and exposed government as illegitimate. WikiLeaks and the similar-minded hacker group Anonymous have made it possible to gain unprecedented insights into the political process and fueled movements that are creating a new common morality, urging people to reclaim their lives and stand up against special interests. The strength of these new movements is the lack of leaders. Instead they rely on individuals acting together without the constraints of tired and corrupted hierarchies.*

In mid-September [2011], Occupy Wall Street [OWS] began in downtown Manhattan. For over a century, Wall Street has represented wealth and political power. Now, the streets of the financial district that only months before gleamed with the facade of enduring capitalism were flooded by 'occupiers', revealing the truth behind the broken promises of equal opportunity and corrupt excess of corporate America.

Here were people from all walks of life, foreclosed and unemployed, students with debts and those who struggle with a pay-or-die medical system. As the people marched with a mixture of jubilation and outrage against the plutocratic takeover of power, the glorified spectacle of the American Dream crumbled in the background.

## Standing up for Free Speech

No one can deny that the Occupy Movement struck a chord with the rank and file of America as it quickly spread nationwide. A couple months in, students at UC [University of California] Berkeley pitched tents on the Mario Savio steps in front of Sproul Hall. When UC police came to dismantle the tents, students linked arms, standing up for their right to freely express themselves. Facing them, armed police violently jabbed them with sticks. This contrast became obvious to the world immediately as the YouTube video of the police attack went viral.

Days later, public outcry against the brutal Cal police action built strong momentum for the movement. During the Mario Savio Memorial Lecture, Occupy Cal exploded in numbers. Thousands of students and protesters gathered outside Sproul Hall in a scene reminiscent of 60's Berkeley. We were witnessing the revival of the Free Speech Movement.

People began to acknowledge that Occupy was the biggest social movement since the anti-war and civil rights protests [of the twentieth century]. The Occupy movement is surely built on past struggles and traditions of activism, yet there is something unique here that was not present in previous movements. So how is this different now than the Civil Rights Movement or even the more recent protests against the WTO [World Trade Organization] and G20 [Group of 20 Finance Ministers and Central Bank Governors]?

In my article, "The Rise of the Occupy Insurgency, the World First Internet Revolution," I explored the role of the Internet in recent revolutions around the world. Although social media and online connection has had significant impact on the birth of the Arab spring and Occupy Movement, there is something else that sets them apart from all that came before.

---

*The Occupy movement is surely built on past struggles and traditions of activism, yet there is something unique here that was not present in previous movements.*

---

## The Influence of WikiLeaks

There is no doubt that the rise of WikiLeaks, the world's first stateless, non-aligned media entity triggered deep political changes on a global scale. Their actions exposed the tyranny and systematic subversion of justice that has become the norm within the global political economy. This small non-profit entity challenged the near total failure of traditional journalism that has mostly served entrenched power. Yet, a less noticed aspect of WikiLeaks's impact lies in its effect on uprisings around the world.

Nov. 28th [2011] marked the one-year anniversary of the WikiLeaks Cablegate release. The US embassy cables revealed deep-seated corruption and illegitimacy of many Middle Eastern dictatorships. Constitutional attorney and author Glenn Greenwald acknowledged the significance of the Wikileaks US State Dept. documents and the impact of these cables on the recent uprisings in Tunisia and Egypt. In reflecting on the past year, Amnesty International noted the role of the leaked documents in triggering these revolutions:

The year 2010 may well be remembered as a watershed year when activists and journalists used new technology to speak truth to power and, in so doing, pushed for greater respect for human rights.

Direct connection through social media and wireless technology helped spread this information and confirmed people's suspicions, sparking a transformation of pervasive defeatism and despair into collective action in the streets. And further, this influence has stretched into the current Occupy Movement. . . .

Now from the Middle East to Spain and Greece and the London riots to the current Occupy movement, we are seeing the waves of action for self-determination reaching the West. After the rise of WikiLeaks, the social and political climate has fundamentally changed. What is different in this WikiLeaks era? It is nothing less than a total shift in consciousness. Beneath the surface of events, a new way of thinking is emerging and changing how people relate to one another.

---

*Now from the Middle East to Spain and Greece and the London riots to the current Occupy movement, we are seeing the waves of action for self-determination reaching the West.*

---

## Power Shifts

As noted, there are similarities between the Occupy Movement and struggles in the past. One common thread is that they start as resistance, opposing injustice. For instance, the Civil Rights Movement was waged against the racist application of law that denied basic human rights for blacks. The Battle of Seattle tried to stop the undemocratic and exploitative economic structures of the WTO. The Occupy Movement also express deep distrust and anger regarding inequality and the global oligarchy's rampant looting of the populace. Yet there is something new unfolding.

It's too early to tell what direction Occupy will go as it just had its three month anniversary [in December 2011]. But, in the big picture, there is an undeniable shift in power dynamics. Resistance is a condition that assumes a lack of power. People are no longer simply resisting. During a general assembly at Occupy Oakland, a man spoke of how there is a difference between revolution and reform. He said that the Occupy Movement is clearly calling for revolution. While social movements in the past involved people making demands of their leaders, this one is bypassing said 'leaders', because they are seen as irreversibly corrupted by a system that is rotten to the core. This movement has been criticized by mainstream media for lack of specific demands for reform, but many see this as its inherent strength. It is clear that people are saying and doing things that only a few years ago would have been inconceivable. The level of creativity and autonomy of this movement indicates something very new is afoot.

Occupiers are not just sitting and waiting for politicians to deliver change. They are taking action, moving their money to credit unions, feeding one another, creating their own media and sorting out how to live together without corporate or political influence.

What makes the Occupy Movement different is this change in perception about the basic illegitimacy of current government and the sense of the individuals' capacity to give direction to their own lives. This combination brought an avalanche of global awakening. Now people are starting to communicate about the root causes of oppression and injustice and bringing new solutions to the table. . . .

## A Global Allegiance

We now know that what is decimating our cities and economies is wholesale fraud by institutions and empirical oligarchs. One inside trader confessed the fact that "Governments don't rule the world, Goldman Sachs does." But, what is changing is that a majority of the people are starting to realize what is happening in their country is also happening in Greece, Iceland, India, Egypt and all around the world.

This type of transnational allegiance is also a guiding force behind the loosely tied online collective Anonymous. 2011 was a year when Anonymous came to the forefront of the public eye. Guy Fawkes masks [from the film *V for Vendetta*, representing the 17th-century Spanish revolutionary] have become powerful symbols that transcend race, color and nationality, embodying a sense of shared morals and ideals popping up on the streets and Internet screens around the world. [As the character V from the film says:]

> ... something unexpected is happening. . . . We are questioning the old assumptions that we are made to consume not to create, that the world was made for our taking, that wars are inevitable, that poverty is unavoidable. As we learn more about our global community a fundamental truth has been rediscovered: We are not so different as we may seem. Every human has strengths, weaknesses, and deep emotions. We crave love, love laughter, fear being alone and dream for a better life.

---

*One inside trader confessed the fact that "Governments don't rule the world, Goldman Sachs does."*

---

Anonymous is tapping into a future for mankind where people form legion with others around the world first and their local regions second. In this sense, Anonymous is a kind of precursor to a world beyond the nation-state, embracing 'festive citizenship'. WikiLeaks and Anonymous have this in common; they are founded on the ability to transcend borders. They both commit to free flow of transnational communication and an open source approach to political power. Similarly, the Occupy Movement quickly spread around the world within weeks, creating simultaneous actions in multiple cities. They did this by using open source methods and direct online connection for mutual support.

## Toward a Common Morality

It is very hard for authoritarians to fight this trans-border movement. It is similar to websites and chat rooms. One can be taken down, but a new one pops up somewhere else to mirror or expand on the original site. In a sense, this is the true force of globalization. On the surface, language and specific solutions might be different, yet people around the world are uniting, standing up for universal rights and a common morality.

After the police brutality in Occupy Oakland, the eyes of the whole world were on one city and it energized the movement. The New York Occupy Wall Street General Assembly pledged to send money and tents while Egyptians in Cairo marched in solidarity. People around the globe watched the livestream of the police raid and eviction of Zuccotti Park and began to see the facade of Western democracy beginning to crumble.

When the Civil Rights Movement took place in the US, it was within the framework of the nation-state. The Battle of Seattle and anti-G20 gatherings protested corporate globalization, yet were always physically held in one city and trapped in an enclosed and blithely insular system. On the other hand, in the Occupy Movement, people are grounded in their locality, but connected globally. One OWS participant said:

> . . . wherever you are in your community is where you occupy. You go to your community, there is Occupy Brooklyn, Occupy Harlem, Occupy the Bronx, Occupy North Carolina. . . . That's what Occupy is about. It's not about Occupy Wall Street, its about Occupy everything.

## Reclaiming Their Own Lives

They are staying right where they are, reclaiming their own cities, enacting general assemblies, while staying in touch with

inspiring collective efforts worldwide. Occupiers are now joining foreclosed homeowners to occupy their own houses. After
serving in the military overseas, veterans like Scott Olson are
now truly serving their country in the Occupy Movement. . . .

With foreclosures and unemployment running rampant,
camp sites are popping up around hundreds of cities. The tent
has become a symbol for this movement. It represents mobile
ideals that take root, rather than a floating thought that comes
and goes. The new-found power of collaboration and allegiance is undeniably transforming the sense of self from an
isolated being with little to offer the world. Now, individuals
are finding new identities as a collaborative beings with the
right to share their impulse for self-determination in a direct
way. . . .

---

*Occupiers are now joining foreclosed homeowners to
occupy their own houses.*

---

What has happened all around the world in the last year
[2011] is that people are challenging . . . hierarchical structures of power that deny a way of knowing informed by their
own experience. In the Occupy Movement, people are realiz-
ing that recognition from a master (credentialed professional
or perceived authority) is no longer necessary and that one
can become master of one's own life. True power ultimately
streams from within and cannot be granted from outside.
This shift away from the recognition model of identity is both
manifested and fostered by Anonymous and Occupy
Movement's leaderless principles.

## The Leaderless Principle

This leaderless element has multiple dimensions. On the surface it can appear as a practical question. Compared to the
Civil Rights Movement in the [19]60's, now the old models of
dissent have become less effective. Individuals who rise above

the crowd stick out and more easily become targets of State oppression. A charismatic leader guiding a movement also had more meaning back then. Once those in power detect the head of a movement, what has been incubating underneath as potential is susceptible to subversion. Before information can be mobilized and ideas fully matured, they can be squashed. With previous models of activism, one only needed to take out the spokesperson to kill the unifying message. We saw this with the assassination of Martin Luther King [Jr.] and Malcolm X. The movements then appeared to lose energy and direction once the leaders were gone. Now an organism without a head offers great advantage in mobilizing ideas quickly beneath the radar. Most importantly, it helps distribute power in the hands of many people. There is something beautiful and profoundly symbolic about the Anonymous image of the suited man without a head that conveys the transformation of corporate hierarchy into a space for true human community.

## Becoming Their Own Leaders

Beyond the practical necessity, the structure of having more than one spokesperson indicates a move away from a recognition model of identity. More people are coming to realize that everyone can tap into their own power and fully count themselves in to become their own leaders in concert with others. For instance, take a look at the phenomenon of the People's Mic. In a corporate system, a microphone represents an amplification of ego and activation of individual power. In most cases, as with the celebrity culture, access to this position is limited to those already endowed by the system with that privilege. The People's Mic on the other hand is inherently communal by using a sound system of simple amplification of an echoing choral human voice. It decentralizes power and gives space for everyone to equally speak within an immediately empathic feedback loop.

Like retweeting in the direct democracy of social media, instead of one voice dominating discourse, diverse views are invited in, echoed and amplified in authentic resonance toward dialogue. This is a philosophy that works to counter the celebrity worship of the individual and hierarchical distribution of power. It is also another essential aspect of Anonymous culture; acknowledging empathic connection and collaborative effort out of shared ideals, rather than an anointed leader held above all others. Whether consciously or not, this Anonymous ethic has served as a model for the OWS movement. Instead of following false gods like Donald Trump, Paris Hilton and puppet politicians, people can now turn inward or to each other to amplify the source of creative power—the human being that speaks and acts in resonance with his fellow man.

---

*More people are coming to realize that everyone can tap into their own power and fully count themselves in to become their own leaders in concert with others.*

---

This emerging leaderless culture is a gradual moving away from the desire for recognition at the center and toward the realization that individual power is not conditioned or determined by outside authority. It is a reorganizing social principle that totally redefines power.

## Redefining Power

So how did WikiLeaks contribute to this power shift? WikiLeaks, as an activist organization was built on an uncompromising commitment to justice. On Nov. 26 [2011] the organization was given the Walkley award, the Australian equivalent of the Pulitzer for excellence in journalism. The panel noted the group's "courageous and controversial commitment to the finest traditions of journalism: justice through transparency."

Julian Assange, the founder of WikiLeaks has become a center of focus in the public eye. Yet, if we look deeply at what is unprecedented about this journalistic and activist enterprise, we can see that this organization is also based on a kind of mutuality similar to the working of Anonymous. It is not really one person leading the charge. One side of their operation depends on a rigorous and innovative approach to technology. Western society has increasingly become lawless when it comes to checks on power of those with money. On the other hand, WikiLeaks by applying the best laws around the world has developed an infrastructure and approach that bypasses established national political controls that stifle dissent or free flow of crucial information. The other side of the WikiLeaks equation are those whistleblowers who have the moral courage to step forward and expose injustice. Needless to say, without the technical foundation and global platform, the organization could not function. But, it is also true that without dissenters inside the system and support from the general public, WikiLeaks success would not have been possible. Neither alleged whistleblower Bradley Manning [US soldier accused of leaking restricted material] nor Julian Assange could have changed history without the other. It is the individual's simple commitment to justice when linked with other's passion that in this case made the difference, transforming technology in service to our higher humanity.

The source of this power is the courage and commitment to justice demonstrated by a person like Manning. When one accesses this commitment within themselves, fear begins to dissolve, as it cannot co-exist with real courage. When WikiLeaks was met with the financial blockade by PayPal, VISA and MasterCard, Anonymous stepped forward to defend what they saw as an attack on the principle of free speech. Truly, what they were defending was the courage to stand up and fight such intrenched power. The morals and ideals that are so vital to a healthy society have steadily been eroded. By turning the tide of technology, these morals are now receiving a new breath of life.

## Exposing Corruption

WikiLeaks is based on the conviction that when corruption of powerful organizations is exposed to the public, there is potential for great change. Leaks driven by conscience can become a kind of explosive compassion which opens systems that have been closed and contaminated with corruption and apathy. In the past, governments and corporations could hide their actions behind smooth rhetoric and propaganda. Now citizens equipped with cell phones and cameras surround those who oppress and then leak or share the actual footage immediately to the world to witness. It is the basic math of social change that says the more unjust actions are witnessed by a certain percentage of the populace, the more people will realize the true state of governments and powerful institutions.

Continued crackdowns in Egypt and now Occupy police-state responses throughout America are exposing governments with their true colors of oppression. The delusional facade of illegitimate authority covering interlocking patronage networks is quickly crumbling before the eyes of the world. The more police and military attack innocent people, the more the thin veil of false power is exposed. A video of a crackdown goes viral on the internet and in the next few days the crowd multiplies with solidarity across borders. We saw examples of this in Occupy Wall Street and Oakland where after brutal raids, the people are more united and committed and so the protest grows.

What happens when the facade of legitimacy begins to fall? People recognize the real source of power is actually within themselves and they start to find their own moral authority. This is what we are witnessing with Occupy Movements and popular uprisings around the world. Berkeley professor Robert Reich, who was a keynote speaker at Mario Savio memorial lecture, said to the thousands gathered, "Moral outrage is the beginning. The days of apathy are over, folks. And once it has begun it cannot be stopped and it will not be stopped."

# 7

# The Occupy Protesters Are Inspired by the Civil Rights Movement

*Andrea Ball*

*Andrea Ball is a reporter at the* Austin American Statesman *and the recipient of a Rosalynn Carter Fellowship for Mental Health Journalism.*

*Many detractors have pointed to vague goals and an overly diverse field of protesters within the Occupy Movement, but many movements have started with vague objectives and developed more stringent demands later. And diversity is a not a detriment but a hallmark of the nationwide protests, showing that many segments of society are fed up with the status quo and demanding change. While the future of the movement is yet unclear, occupiers have given underprivileged Americans a voice.*

There were babies and seniors, students and retirees, the dreadlocked and carefully coiffed. And there, on the fringes of the protest in front of Austin City Hall, was Trish Pulsipher.

The office manager had used her lunch break Thursday [October 6, 2011] to check out the first day of Occupy Austin, the local spinoff of a national protest against the influence of corporate money in politics and the growing wealth gap. Pulsipher, 32, seemed pleased watching the crowd energetically chant, talk, laugh, snap pictures and make posters. But one thought nagged at her: What if people stop protesting?

"It's a little bit scary to think it might be all over tomorrow," said Pulsipher, who works for an engineering firm in Pflugerville. "But I don't think it will."

The protest drew more than 1,000 people Thursday [October 6, 2011] and continued Friday outside City Hall, with several hundred people marching to the downtown Bank of America branch on Congress Avenue.

## Gaining Momentum

Local organizers say it will continue for weeks. But as the Occupy movement gained momentum this week—popping up in cities across the nation and abroad—it was still unclear whether the protests were a passing fad, a flash of national frustration destined to fizzle. Some critics call the effort unfocused, unrealistic and hypocritical as many of the protesters benefit from corporate jobs and products.

Others say the protests show all the hallmarks of a lasting, bona fide movement.

"I think that is what's unfolding before our very eyes," said Janet Davis, an associate professor in the department of American studies at the University of Texas. "There is definitely something in the air."

The Occupy movement began in New York on Sept. 17 [2011], when about 1,000 people marched through the city's financial district. The national media paid scant attention to the Wall Street demonstrations until Oct. 1, when more than 700 protesters were arrested while trying to cross the Brooklyn Bridge. Since then, the Occupy movement has spread to dozens of cities, including Philadelphia, Miami, Chicago, Boston and Memphis, Tenn. On Thursday, protests began in Dallas, San Antonio and Houston.

## Vague Objectives

Although Occupy Austin has developed its own priorities—including tax reforms for the wealthy and limits on contributions to political campaigns—diffuse grievances and vague demands have characterized the national movement from the beginning. Protesters in front of City Hall, as elsewhere, have decried a range of issues and institutions, including student debt, standardized testing, greed, war, the Federal Reserve, corporations and Wall Street. Meanwhile, Occupy Wall Street says it has no official list of demands.

That lack of focus is a detriment to the movement's success, according to an article by Daniel Indiviglio, an associate editor at *The Atlantic.*

---

*Protesters in front of City Hall, as elsewhere, have decried a range of issues and institutions, including student debt, standardized testing, greed, war, the Federal Reserve, corporations and Wall Street.*

---

"Any protest that hopes to accomplish some goal needs, well, a goal," he wrote this week. "If a demonstration like this lacks concrete objectives, then its purpose will be limited at best and nonexistent at worst."

Others say the early stages of social movements, including the civil rights movement and the tea party, are often marked by vague objectives.

"Indeed, they have to if they want to bring in a broad array of participants," said T.V. Reed, author of *The Art of Protest: Culture and Activism from the Civil Rights Movement to the Streets of Seattle.*

"As movements start to feel their power, and to understand precisely where they can exert that power, their goals and objectives become clearer," Reed said.

## Grassroots Growth

Another hallmark of a true social movement is grass-roots support that spreads to other areas, Davis said. One example: the 1960 sit-ins over segregation at Woolworth's department store lunch counters.

On Feb. 5, 1960, four African American college students in Greensboro, N.C., sat down at the lunch counter and ordered coffee. They were refused service. Over the next few days, crowds of other people joined the protest. It then spread to other cities across the South.

On July 25, 1960, the Greensboro Woolworth's ended the segregation of its lunch counters. The entire Woolworth's chain followed suit the next day.

Like those protests, the Occupy rallies seem to be growing organically and spreading rapidly, Davis said.

"The act of occupying space is a really powerful part of making a claim to the democratic process," she said.

---

*"Students have time and the energy of youth; unions have monetary resources and the stability that comes with an older constituency."*

---

Support from a range of people and organizations is also important, Reed said. The Wall Street group, for example, has been endorsed by the Transit Workers Union and the United Federation of Teachers. In Austin, labor group Education Austin and advocates for homeless people have offered their support.

"Students have time and the energy of youth; unions have monetary resources and the stability that comes with an older constituency," said Reed, a professor at Washington State University. "This combination nearly brought down the government of France in 1968 and was at the heart of the protests against unjust forms of globalization in Seattle in 1999."

## Diverse Protesters

Some conservative commentators dismiss the protests as a collection of bored youths who will soon lose interest.

To be sure, the Occupy Austin movement has attracted stereotypical liberal protesters: students, old hippies and young people with tattoos, dreadlocks and wildly colored hair.

Huston-Tillotson University biology student Teegan Mullins was among those holding signs in front of City Hall, where passing drivers regularly blared their horns in support. The 22-year-old, who works at her parents' chicken farm in Dripping Springs, said she came out because she's upset about the economy.

"There's so much frustration that's been building," she said. "I hope something gets done."

But the Occupy Austin crowd has also been populated with many other kinds of people, including retirees and workers who arrived later in the evening.

Nancy Smith, 55, said she doesn't usually participate in such events. But since moving to Austin two years ago [in 2009], she's been hit hard by the economy. Unable to find a teaching job, she said she's scraped by grading tests for an educational company and handing out food samples at a grocery store.

She and her husband, who lost his job as an architect, have burned through their savings, she said.

"This isn't about being a radical or overthrowing the government," Smith said. "It's about middle-class people like myself."

Bonnie Wences, who attended Occupy Austin's opening protest, said she doesn't know where this is all going. But the 56-year-old Austinite, who lost her job in corporate retail and is now making minimum wage at a job program through AARP [American Association of Retired Persons], said that, if nothing else, being able to protest is cathartic.

"Sometimes we need people to listen to us, to get it out," she said. "That's important, too."

# 8

# The Occupy Movement Is Based on Anarchist Principles

*David Graeber*

*David Graeber is an American anthropologist and anarchist who currently holds the position of Reader in Social Anthropology at Goldsmiths, University of London. He is a social and political activist, member of the labor union Industrial Workers of the World, and an early participant of Occupy Wall Street. Graeber has written numerous books, among them* Direct Action: an Ethnography; Debt: the First 5,000 Years; *and* Revolutions in Reverse.

*The protests of the Occupy Movement have embraced anarchism in its most peaceful and tolerant form, refusing to recognize existing political institutions, the legitimacy of the existing legal order, and internal hierarchies. While anarchy is often associated with lawlessness and violence, the Occupy Movement understands its true heritage, exercising peaceful direct action. Instead of accepting the current political situation, it strives for real democracy, where tolerance and civil rights are honored and citizen's lives are not threatened by armies, police, and prisons.*

Almost every time I'm interviewed by a mainstream journalist about Occupy Wall Street [OWS] I get some variation of the same lecture:

How are you going to get anywhere if you refuse to create a leadership structure or make a practical list of demands? And what's with all this anarchist nonsense—the consensus, the sparkly fingers? Don't you realise all this radical language is going to alienate people? You're never going to be able to reach regular, mainstream Americans with this sort of thing!

## An Anarchist Movement

If one were compiling a scrapbook of worst advice ever given, this sort of thing might well merit an honourable place. After all, since the financial crash of 2007, there have been dozens of attempts to kick-off a national movement against the depredations of the United States' financial elites taking the approach such journalists recommended. All failed. It was only on August 2 [2011], when a small group of anarchists and other anti-authoritarians showed up at a meeting called by one such group and effectively wooed everyone away from the planned march and rally to create a genuine democratic assembly, on basically anarchist principles, that the stage was set for a movement that Americans from Portland to Tuscaloosa were willing to embrace.

*History has shown that vast inequalities of wealth, institutions like slavery, debt peonage or wage labour, can only exist if backed up by armies, prisons, and police.*

I should be clear here what I mean by "anarchist principles". The easiest way to explain anarchism is to say that it is a political movement that aims to bring about a genuinely free society—that is, one where humans only enter those kinds of relations with one another that would not have to be enforced by the constant threat of violence. History has shown that vast inequalities of wealth, institutions like slavery, debt peonage or wage labour, can only exist if backed up by armies, prisons, and police. Anarchists wish to see human relations that would not have to be backed up by armies, prisons and police. Anarchism envisions a society based on equality and solidarity, which could exist solely on the free consent of participants.

## Anarchism Versus Marxism

Traditional Marxism, of course, aspired to the same ultimate goal but there was a key difference. Most Marxists insisted that it was necessary first to seize state power, and all the mechanisms of bureaucratic violence that come with it, and use them to transform society—to the point where, they argued such mechanisms would, ultimately, become redundant and fade away. Even back in the 19th century, anarchists argued that this was a pipe dream. One cannot, they argued, create peace by training for war, equality by creating top-down chains of command, or, for that matter, human happiness by becoming grim joyless revolutionaries who sacrifice all personal self-realisation or self-fulfillment to the cause.

It's not just that the ends do not justify the means (though they don't), you will never achieve the ends at all unless the means are themselves a model for the world you wish to create. Hence the famous anarchist call to begin "building the new society in the shell of the old" with egalitarian experiments ranging from free schools to radical labour unions to rural communes.

## Moving Away from Violence

Anarchism was also a revolutionary ideology, and its emphasis on individual conscience and individual initiative meant that during the first heyday of revolutionary anarchism between roughly 1875 and 1914, many took the fight directly to heads of state and capitalists, with bombings and assassinations. Hence the popular image of the anarchist bomb-thrower. It's worthy of note that anarchists were perhaps the first political movement to realise that terrorism, even if not directed at innocents, doesn't work. For nearly a century now, in fact, anarchism has been one of the very few political philosophies whose exponents never blow anyone up (indeed, the 20th-century political leader who drew most from the anarchist tradition was Mohandas K. Gandhi.)

---

*Direct action is, ultimately, the defiant insistence on acting as if one is already free.*

---

Yet for the period of roughly 1914 to 1989, a period during which the world was continually either fighting or preparing for world wars, anarchism went into something of an eclipse for precisely that reason: To seem "realistic", in such violent times, a political movement had to be capable of organising armies, navies and ballistic missile systems, and that was one thing at which Marxists could often excel. But everyone recognised that anarchists—rather to their credit—would never be able to pull it off. It was only after 1989, when the age of great war mobilisations seemed to have ended, that a global revolutionary movement based on anarchist principles—the global justice movement—promptly reappeared.

How, then, did OWS embody anarchist principles? It might be helpful to go over this point by point:

*The refusal to recognise the legitimacy of existing political institutions.* One reason for the much-discussed refusal to issue demands is because issuing demands means recognising the legitimacy—or at least, the power—of those of whom the demands are made. Anarchists often note that this is the difference between protest and direct action: Protest, however militant, is an appeal to the authorities to behave differently; direct action, whether it's a matter of a community building a well or making salt in defiance of the law (Gandhi's example again), trying to shut down a meeting or occupy a factory, is a matter of acting as if the existing structure of power does not even exist. Direct action is, ultimately, the defiant insistence on acting as if one is already free.

*The refusal to accept the legitimacy of the existing legal order.* The second principle, obviously, follows from the first. From the very beginning, when we first started holding planning meetings in Tompkins Square Park in New York, organisers knowingly ignored local ordinances that insisted that any gathering of more than 12 people in a public park is illegal without police permission—simply on the grounds that such laws should not exist. On the same grounds, of course, we chose to occupy a park, inspired by examples from the Middle East and southern Europe, on the grounds that, as the public, we should not need permission to occupy public space. This might have been a very minor form of civil disobedience but it was crucial that we began with a commitment to answer only to a moral order, not a legal one.

*The refusal to create an internal hierarchy, but instead to create a form of consensus-based direct democracy.* From the very beginning, too, organisers made the audacious decision to operate not only by direct democracy, without leaders, but by consensus. The first decision ensured that there would be no formal leadership structure that could be co-opted or coerced; the second, that no majority could bend a minority to its will, but that all crucial decisions had to be made by general consent. American anarchists have long considered consensus process (a tradition that has emerged from a confluence of feminism, anarchism and spiritual traditions like the Quakers) crucial for the reason that it is the only form of decision-making that could operate without coercive enforcement—since if a majority does not have the means to compel a minority to obey its dictates, all decisions will, of necessity, have to be made by general consent.

*The embrace of prefigurative politics.* As a result, Zuccotti Park [in New York City], and all subsequent encampments, became spaces of experiment with creating the institutions of a new society—not only democratic General Assemblies but kitchens, libraries, clinics, media centres and a host of other institutions, all operating on anarchist principles of mutual aid and self-organisation—a genuine attempt to create the institutions of a new society in the shell of the old.

Why did it work? Why did it catch on? One reason is, clearly, because most Americans are far more willing to embrace radical ideas than anyone in the established media is willing to admit. The basic message—that the American political order is absolutely and irredeemably corrupt, that both parties have been bought and sold by the wealthiest 1 per cent of the population, and that if we are to live in any sort of genuinely democratic society, we're going to have to start from scratch—clearly struck a profound chord in the American psyche.

---

*Democracy meant the madness of crowds: bloody, tumultuous and untenable.*

---

Perhaps this is not surprising: We are facing conditions that rival those of the 1930s, the main difference being that the media seems stubbornly willing to acknowledge it. It raises intriguing questions about the role of the media itself in American society. Radical critics usually assume the "corporate media", as they call it, mainly exists to convince the public that existing institutions are healthy, legitimate and just. It is becoming increasingly apparent that they do not really see this is possible; rather, their role is simply to convince members of an increasingly angry public that no one else has come to the same conclusions they have. The result is an ideology that no one really believes, but most people at least suspect that everybody else does.

Nowhere is this disjunction between what ordinary Americans really think, and what the media and political establishment tells them they think, more clear than when we talk about democracy.

## Democracy in America

According to the official version, of course, "democracy" is a system created by the Founding Fathers, based on checks and balances between president, congress and judiciary. In fact, nowhere in the Declaration of Independence or Constitution does it say anything about the US being a "democracy". The authors of those documents, almost to a man, defined "democracy" as a matter of collective self-governance by popular assemblies, and as such they were dead-set against it.

Democracy meant the madness of crowds: bloody, tumultuous and untenable. "There was never a democracy that didn't commit suicide," wrote [John] Adams: [Alexander] Hamilton justified the system of checks and balances by insisting that it was necessary to create a permanent body of the "rich and well-born" to check the "imprudence" of democracy, or even that limited form that would be allowed in the lower house of representatives.

The result was a republic—modelled not on Athens, but on Rome. It only came to be redefined as a "democracy" in the early 19th century because ordinary Americans had very different views, and persistently tended to vote—those who were allowed to vote—for candidates who called themselves "democrats". But what did—and what do—ordinary Americans mean by the word? Did they really just mean a system where they get to weigh in on which politicians will run the government? It seems implausible. After all, most Americans loathe politicians, and tend to be skeptical about the very idea of government. If they universally hold out "democracy" as their political ideal, it can only be because they still see it, however vaguely, as self-governance—as what the Founding Fathers tended to denounce as either "democracy" or, as they sometimes also put it, "anarchy".

If nothing else, this would help explain the enthusiasm with which they have embraced a movement based on directly democratic principles, despite the uniformly contemptuous dismissal of the United States' media and political class.

## American Roots of Anarchy

In fact, this is not the first time a movement based on fundamentally anarchist principles—direct action, direct democracy, a rejection of existing political institutions and attempt to create alternative ones—has cropped up in the US. The civil rights movement (at least its more radical branches), the antinuclear movement, and the global justice movement all took similar directions. Never, however, has one grown so startlingly quickly. But in part, this is because this time around, the organisers went straight for the central contradiction. They directly challenged the pretenses of the ruling elite that they are presiding over a democracy.

---

*As the history of the past movements all make clear, nothing terrifies those running the US more than the danger of democracy breaking out.*

---

When it comes to their most basic political sensibilities, most Americans are deeply conflicted. Most combine a deep reverence for individual freedom with a near-worshipful identification with institutions like the army and police. Most combine an enthusiasm for markets with a hatred of capitalists. Most are simultaneously profoundly egalitarian, and deeply racist. Few are actual anarchists; few even know what "anarchism" means; it's not clear how many, if they did learn, would ultimately wish to discard the state and capitalism entirely. Anarchism is much more than simply grassroots democracy: It ultimately aims to eliminate all social relations, from wage labour to patriarchy, that can only be maintained by the systematic threat of force.

But one thing overwhelming numbers of Americans do feel is that something is terribly wrong with their country, that its key institutions are controlled by an arrogant elite, that radical change of some kind is long since overdue. They're right. It's hard to imagine a political system so systematically corrupt—one where bribery, on every level, has not only been made legal, but soliciting and dispensing bribes has become the full-time occupation of every American politician. The outrage is appropriate. The problem is that up until September 17, [2011], the only side of the spectrum willing to propose radical solutions of any sort was the Right.

## Direct Action Is a Threat to the Status Quo

As the history of the past movements all make clear, nothing terrifies those running the US more than the danger of democracy breaking out. The immediate response to even a modest spark of democratically organised civil disobedience is a panicked combination of concessions and brutality. How else can one explain the recent national mobilisation of thousands of riot cops, the beatings, chemical attacks, and mass arrests, of citizens engaged in precisely the kind of democratic assemblies the Bill of Rights was designed to protect, and whose only crime—if any—was the violation of local camping regulations?

Our media pundits might insist that if average Americans ever realised the anarchist role in Occupy Wall Street, they would turn away in shock and horror; but our rulers seem, rather, to labour under a lingering fear that if any significant number of Americans do find out what anarchism really is, they might well decide that rulers of any sort are unnecessary.

# 9

# The Occupiers Need to Start a Socialist Revolution

*Jeff Mackler*

*Jeff Mackler has written and lectured widely from a socialist perspective. His numerous books, pamphlets, and articles cover a range of subjects, including revolutionary developments in Latin America, the Cuban Revolution, global warming/climate crisis, health care, trade union struggles, and the fight to build the US antiwar movement. Mackler is National Secretary of Socialist Action and was his party's 2006 candidate for the US Senate in California.*

*The Occupy Movement has exposed the limitations of our current democracy, its underlying injustices, its racism and sexism. As the protests continue, occupiers are learning that reforms are futile, and that the system itself has to be replaced by a new and peaceful socialism. This new system is not based on the corruption and horror of the Stalinist era, but rooted in Karl Marx's writings. As the protests in Egypt and the Middle East have shown, it is not enough to overthrow dictatorship and hope for capitalist reforms. There, as in the United States, capitalism needs to be challenged and replaced with a system that insures freedom and justice for all its citizens.*

At last count 900 U.S. cities have joined the Occupy Wall Street (OWS) movement. Five hundred other cities and towns on every continent have joined the mushrooming mo-

Jeff Mackler, "Occupy Movement Goals: Socialist Revolution or Capitalist Reforms?," *Socialist Action Newspaper Online*, November 2011. InternationalViewpoint.org. Copyright © 2011 by Jeff Mackler. All rights reserved. Reproduced by permission.

bilizations in solidarity. With each repressive blow, the movement comes back stronger—more inclusive, more confident, and more clearly focused.

"The Americans are fighting back at last," cried one European demonstrator, echoing the pride and solidarity felt by people the world over, who understand that they too are the 99 percent—the working masses everywhere who create the wealth and yet are increasingly trampled on by the banking and corporate elite and their ever-distrusted political representatives or dictators.

When New York City's Mayor [Michael] Bloomberg threatened to close down the OWS encampment at Zuccotti Park, he was confronted with an unexpected threat from the AFL-CIO [American Federation of Labor and Congress of Industrial Organization] and its constituent unions, including the Communication Workers of America. The local union officialdom called on its ranks to "defend" the occupiers. "Defend" is a special word in working-class circles. It signifies a massive mobilization against those agents of a repressive society who would employ force and violence against peaceful protesters demanding fundamental change.

Bloomberg backed down when he and his cohorts judged that removing several hundred youthful occupiers would be quite a different proposition from challenging a mobilization of the organized labor movement.

---

*A police-fired missile sent 22-year-old Iraq War veteran Scott Olsen to the hospital with a severe skull fracture.*

---

## Violent Responses to Peaceful Protest

Despite that victory, we can expect that the authorities will attempt to beat back the Occupy movement by repression, if they think they can get away with it. This was seen when, without warning, [in California] Oakland's repressive apparatus was unleashed on Oct. 25, [2011] at 4 a.m. About 900 cops fired rubber bullets and beanbag missiles at close range at some 100 occupiers in Oakland's Frank Ogawa Plaza, adjacent to City Hall. The attack included tear-gas and clubbing the non-violent occupiers.

In the name of sanitation concerns, the police destroyed the encampment, trashing some 100 tents and arresting scores of Oakland's peaceful protesters. A police-fired missile sent 22-year-old Iraq War veteran Scott Olsen to the hospital with a severe skull fracture.

The next day, the Occupy Oakland General Assembly reclaimed the now renamed Oscar Grant Plaza, with some 2000 supporters mobilizing to protest the police attack.

In response to the attack, 1607 participants debated a resolution calling for an Oakland general strike on Wednesday, Nov. 2. The resolution passed by a 96.9% margin. The resolution stated, "Instead of workers going to work and students going to school, the people will converge on downtown Oakland to shut down the city.... All banks and corporations should close down for the day or we will march on them.... The whole world is watching Oakland. Let's show them what is possible."

*Then [in 1946] as now, there was a giant gap between the desire of labor's ranks to struggle and the willingness of labor's blustering misleaders to lead.*

## A Global Movement

Indeed, the whole world was watching the events in Oakland, and solidarity events took place in a number of cities. Occupy Wall Street in New York issued a call for a nationwide show of support on Nov. 2. And a planned march from Tahrir Square to the U.S. Embassy in Cairo, Egypt, included a statement of solidarity with the beleaguered Oakland protesters. It read in part: "The moment that we find ourselves in is nothing new, as we in Egypt and others have been fighting against systems of repression, disenfranchisement and the unchecked ravages of global capitalism (yes, we said it, capitalism): a system that has made a world that is dangerous and cruel to its inhabitants."

Most participants understand that the dramatic call for an Oakland general strike, without mass support from the labor movement, will likely not materialize. Nevertheless, it is encouraging that several unions have called on their members to take part. The expected outpouring of working people and youth in solidarity with Occupy Oakland will represent yet another powerful step toward their mobilization in critical class battles to come.

In 1946, as part of the post-World War II strike wave of industrial workers that engulfed the country in the largest multi-million-member labor mobilization in U.S. history, there was indeed a general strike in Oakland, one of the few in the nation's history. The strike began with the solidarity of local trade unionists who had witnessed the bosses herding scab workers through union picket lines at a department store. But the labor bureaucracy, as today, largely stood aside from what developed, virtually spontaneously, into a 54-hour general strike that closed down the city.

Then as now, there was a giant gap between the desire of labor's ranks to struggle and the willingness of labor's blustering misleaders to lead. But once again, the question of labor's leadership will be posed as rank-and-filers embark on the road to re-capturing their unions from the current crop of pro-capitalist bureaucrats.

In the process, as in 1946, they will take their struggles into the political arena and contemplate the formation of a mass labor party to compliment labor's struggle at the point of production with a political fight against the policies of the twin parties of capital.

## Growing Frustration over Inequality

With each passing day the Occupy movement gathers momentum as it reflects the deep-seated anger at the incursions on the quality of life, standard of living, and basic security of the broad working class and its allies among the oppressed and youth everywhere. This is a movement that in the main rejects the very essence of capitalist functioning worldwide, including its imperial wars and occupations and its outright domination by the billionaire and trillionaire ruling class—the one percent—whose interests are defended without question by the twin capitalist parties that govern in the interests of their corporate and banking overlords.

An October [2011] *New York Times* article tells the story well. Entitled, "New Poll Finds a Deep Distrust of Government," The *Times* poll found that "almost half of the public [a large plurality] thinks that the sentiment at the root of the Occupy Movement generally reflects the views of all Americans." This stands in sharp contrast to an earlier *Times* poll that found that the reactionary Tea Party's views reflects the opinion of some 27 percent.

---

*Occupation activists are learning from bitter experience that the prospect of reforming capitalism is futile and that the system itself, at its roots, must be challenged, defeated, and replaced.*

---

The recent poll found that an astounding "89 percent distrust the government to do the right thing." The article asserted that "a remarkable sense of pessimism and skepticism was apparent in question after question in the survey, which found that Congressional approval had reached a new low of 9 percent."

Despite the mass sentiment and impressive and growing mobilizations against capitalist austerity, however, the official labor movement, as well as the organizations that purport to represent the interests of oppressed nationalities, have yet to exercise their still potent power to challenge and reverse the deepening capitalist offensive.

## The Politics of Fear

Today's labor officialdom, compelled now by rank-and-file pressure to at least posture with a modicum of identification with the Occupy movement, remains, with virtually no exceptions, bound in a deadly alliance with the Democratic Party and the [President Barack] Obama administration. This is despite the fact that the latter has proven to be capitalism's most fervent representative in imposing a level of austerity and war that the previous [George W.] Bush administration never dreamed of.

For the ruling-class rich, and their twin political parties in the United States, there is no alternative to saving their degenerating social system other than continued austerity, cutbacks of every sort, imperialist wars of plunder and occupation, catastrophic assaults of the environment and the promotion of racist, sexist, and anti-immigrant hysteria aimed at dividing the working class to pit one sector against another.

Increasing numbers of Occupation activists are learning from bitter experience that the prospect of reforming capitalism is futile and that the system itself, at its roots, must be challenged, defeated, and replaced. In an ongoing process that combines mass actions, political discussion, and debate, socialist solutions are being considered to a degree not seen in a generation or more.

Socialism is a new social order where for the first time in human history the working masses rule in their own name, as opposed to the elite capitalist property owners and the governments they select to advance their own interests at the expense of us all.

This is not the bureaucratic caricature of socialism that existed in the [Josef] Stalin era and that prevailed in the former [Union of Soviet Socialist Republics] USSR and Eastern Europe before it was challenged and overthrown by its victims, but the dynamic, democratic, and revolutionary socialism pioneered by Karl Marx and Frederick Engels—as well as by Vladimir Lenin and Leon Trotsky and other early leaders of the historic 1917 Russian Revolution.

The socialist revolution in Russia was one in which the working-class majority ruled society in their own interests, and through their own institutions, in order to prioritize human needs in every social arena. The revolutionary government was based on the political and economic rule of mass working-class assemblies or councils of workers and the oppressed ("Soviets" in the Russian language). This was a deep-going revolution that abolished the capitalist system of private ownership of society's productive machinery, banks, and resources that had been previously organized to extract the wealth created by the people in the interests of the vast profits of the few.

## Socialist Revolution Is Necessary

No ruling-class minority in human history, from the time of the ancient slave societies of the Greeks and Romans thousands of years ago, to the centuries of feudal monarchies, and to today's capitalist property-owning elite, has ever relinquished its power voluntarily. Socialist revolution, in the only true sense of the term, is the conscious organization and mobilization of the vast majority to challenge the rulers for power. To envision such a massive social transformation is impossible without the direct involvement of working people acting as a conscious class alternative to the present reactionary and minority social order.

It is no coincidence that the Egyptian people's removal of the hated Hosni Mubarak dictatorship, beginning with the massive assemblies at Tahrir Square, served to inspire the original OWS activists in the U.S. But Mubarak's forced departure was only the beginning of an ongoing revolutionary process. Egyptian capitalism, however discredited, remains in place and along with it a military regime that still rules with terror and has failed in virtually every respect to substantially change the lives of the Egyptian people.

The dictatorship of capital also remains in Tunisia and ever more so in Libya, where U.S./NATO [North Atlantic Treaty Organization] military forces exchanged their previously favored [Muammar] Gadhafi dictatorship with another, even more intimately tied to imperialism. None of the deep social problems plaguing those countries will be solved short of a socialist revolution.

---

*[T]he Egyptian people's removal of the hated Hosni Mubarak dictatorship, beginning with the massive assemblies at Tahrir Square, served to inspire the original [occupy] activists in the U.S.*

---

## Challenging Capitalism

History has demonstrated that the construction of a mass revolutionary socialist party, rooted in the struggles of the masses everywhere and dedicated to the total re-organization of society to establish working-class power, is a prerequisite to any successful challenge to the capitalist order.

In the United States, Socialist Action strives to be part of the critical process of building such a revolutionary socialist party. Socialist Action's "Workers' Action Program to Fight the Crisis" is aimed at mobilizing millions around specific and realistic demands to challenge the capitalist offensive and, in time, the capitalist order itself.

# 10

# The Occupiers Need to Mobilize Students and Unions to Succeed

## Laird Harrison and Michelle Nichols

*Laird Harrison is a novelist and multimedia journalist. He has worked as a correspondent for* TIME *and* People *magazines and has written for many national magazines and newspapers, including* Audubon, Health, *the* San Francisco Chronicle, *and the* Cleveland Plain Dealer. *He has produced video for websites, including* Smithsonianmag.com, *and audio for WUNC radio. Harrison has also recently completed work on an interactive novel,* Fallen Lake. *Michelle Nichols is a reporter for the international news agency Reuters.*

*In an effort to keep the momentum going, the Occupy Movement has set its sights on influencing the upcoming presidential elections with rallies and protests, changing the fabric of national banking, and becoming an even greater presence online—from social media to international news outlets. By refusing to establish traditional hierarchies, the protesters are hoping to influence American society and change a system they deem corrupt and driven by greed and injustice.*

It's been a long, cold winter already for Occupy Wall Street, the protest movement that burst onto the scene in September [2011] to focus national attention on income inequality and the perceived greed of the rich and powerful.

Laird Harrison and Michelle Nichols, "Occupy 2012: Movement Struggles To Evolve, Maintain Momentum," *The Huffington Post Online*, January 9, 2012. HuffingtonPost .com. Copyright © 2012 by Thomson Reuters. All rights reserved. Reproduced by permission.

Police have cleared the signature "Occupy" encampments in New York, Los Angeles, Oakland and other major cities. Cold weather, and perhaps protest fatigue, have weakened the handful of camps that remain around the country. The lack of a coherent set of demands has made it difficult for the young movement to affect policy or otherwise score victories that might keep recruits coming.

But the movement has clearly influenced the national political conversation, with even President Barack Obama echoing some of its themes in calling for a "fair shot" and "fair share" for all.

Now, as Occupy heads into 2012, participants in the leaderless movement are developing a range of new strategies and tactics to keep what they view as the injustices of the economic system in the spotlight.

Here are some ways the Occupy movement is trying to evolve:

## Occupy the Election

Occupy has been likened to the conservative Tea Party movement, which emerged in 2009 and helped elect dozens of Republicans. But many in the Occupy movement specifically reject electoral politics, which they see as hopelessly tainted by money. Relationships with labor unions, the natural allies of Occupy when it comes to electoral politics, have been a mixed bag, with some unions, notably National Nurses United, strongly backing the protesters while others have kept their distance.

In the current election cycles, it appears the main Occupy activities will be rallies, sit-ins, and heckling candidates on the stump. During the Iowa caucus campaign, a handful of occupiers interrupted speeches by [Barack] Obama and by Republican presidential candidates Newt Gingrich and Ron Paul. Small groups also targeted New Jersey Governor Chris Christie as he campaigned for Gingrich's rival Mitt Romney, and stuck

Romney himself, who got rich as a private equity investor, with the moniker "Mr. One Percent." New Hampshire campaign events have similarly been a target of small groups of protesters.

---

*Some groups of protesters are trying to come up with alternative banking systems.*

---

## Occupy the Economy

The Occupy movement blames the banks for the worst U.S. recession in decades. And one of its more successful initiatives has been a campaign urging consumers to move their money from the commercial banks to not-for-profit credit unions; in a little over a month, credit unions pulled in hundreds of thousands of new customers. Bank of America also scrapped a widely criticized $5 monthly fee for debit cards, which the Occupy movement claimed as a victory. Occupy San Francisco is planning a big demonstration in that city's Financial District on Jan 20 [2012].

Some groups of protesters are trying to come up with alternative banking systems. Others are pushing for legislation. Protesters in Oakland and San Francisco have carried placards calling for a return to the Depression-era Glass-Steagall Act, which separated investment banking and commercial banking. Occupy the SEC [Securities and Exchange Commission], a committee of Occupy Wall Street, is calling for tough implementation of the so-called Volcker Rule, which would bar U.S. banks from using depositor's funds for speculative investments.

On the West Coast, demonstrators have twice picketed at ports, shutting down shipping terminals for up to 24 hours. But truckers, stevedores and longshoremen who refused to cross picket lines lost pay, raising the question of whom the action was helping, or hurting. The International Longshore and Warehouse Union publicly opposed the Dec. 12 [2012] action that aimed to shut down ports, while the International Brotherhood of Teamsters took a neutral stance.

Judging from the history of social movements, Occupy's relationship with labor unions, as well as students, could ultimately be the key to its influence, says Robert Cohen, a professor of history and social studies at New York University.

"It has to be large-scale to continue to demonstrate force," he said. "It has to bring together more allied groups. And someone has to push this into specific policies."

## Occupy Housing

In December [2011] protesters launched Occupy Our Homes, a bid to take back foreclosed homes. Occupiers took up residence in a home in Oakland, California, and one in Brooklyn, New York, that day, demanding that lenders renegotiate mortgages for the homeowners. National Occupy Our Homes organizer Matt Browner Hamlin said protesters had set a goal of over 100 such "actions" around the country in the next few months.

---

*The Occupy movement has been driven by social media, and activists are now moving to build on their successful use of* Facebook, Twitter *and* YouTube *with new tools and technology.*

---

The Atlanta group is already claiming victory; Occupy Atlanta member Tom Franzen says it forced JPMorgan Chase to offer more generous terms to homeowner Birgitte Walker, who ran into financial difficulties after being honorably discharged from the Army. Chase acknowledges that it modified Walker's loan, but spokesperson Nancy Norris said protesters had nothing to do with it. "We had been working with her for a year," she said.

Elsewhere, the Occupy Our Homes movement has run into stiff resistance. Just before New Year's Eve, police arrested squatters in an Oakland home they were holding "as collateral." It was the second time police had driven Oakland occupiers from a private residence, suggesting that squatting in homes may be just as challenging as camping in parks.

## Occupy Cyberspace

The Occupy movement has been driven by social media, and activists are now moving to build on their successful use of *Facebook, Twitter* and *YouTube* with new tools and technology. The group rolled out *StudioOccupy.org*, which allows protesters to easily share and edit videos and other multimedia presentations online. *Occupydream.org* aims to collect a million "statements of dreams" in advance of a march on Washington timed for Martin Luther King's birthday on Jan. 16.

Some protesters have also begun to use "Vibe," an application for iPhones, iPads and Android that allows the user to send messages that are only visible to other users, and not to police or other outsiders. Vibe messages are anonymous, and users can control how far they are broadcast (from 150 feet to worldwide) and for how long (the messages disappear after a set time period ranging from 15 minutes to 30 days, leaving no trail).

The use of such technology enables the movement to mobilize and organize efficiently without a top-down hierarchy. Social movements in the past required a leader to put out orders to lieutenants who passed them along to the foot soldiers, but now any individual can call a protest at any time, with the crowd deciding on the spur of the moment whose call to action deserves attention.

## Occupy Real Space

Police raids on the big metropolitan camps created the appearance that all occupy camps were evicted. But tent communities have quietly persisted.

While no official count exists, *Firedoglake*, a news website sympathetic to the movement, counted 65 tent communities in the United States that were expected to last through the winter. Perhaps the most visible, an Occupy DC camp in Washington's McPherson Square, a couple of blocks from the White House, has weatherized its tents and obtained winter sleeping bags.

Other occupiers have moved indoors. Occupy Wall Street is renting office space in lower Manhattan, and Occupy Atlanta is in the top floor of a homeless shelter. Evicted campers have not all abandoned their former spaces either: on New Year's Eve, hundreds of people gathered at Zuccotti Park in lower Manhattan, where the largest Occupy camp once stood, and 68 were arrested when they tried to remove police barricades.

---

*Chants like "Whose streets? Our streets" and "banks got bailed out, we got sold out" were suddenly as familiar as snatches of Bob Dylan songs were to a previous generation of protesters.*

---

Questions about physical space have stimulated a debate within the movement. Some argue that camps are essential as bases for operations, as dramatic symbols or as model egalitarian communities. Others say housekeeping and organizational challenges in the camps have drained the group's energy away from more effective tactics for social change. But most predicted that spring would find a new blooming of tent communities around the country.

## Occupy Culture

The protesters' slogan "We are the 99 percent," which refers to a view that the richest 1 percent have a virtual monopoly on money, power and influence, has struck a chord across the country, and the movement's rhetoric has quickly become a part of popular culture. Occupy this, occupy that—there are few examples of a single word jumping so quickly from the middle pages of the dictionary to the forefront of public conversation. Chants like "Whose streets? Our streets" and "banks got bailed out, we got sold out" were suddenly as familiar as snatches of Bob Dylan songs were to a previous generation of protesters.

But Occupy protesters have a much more ambitious cultural agenda. In the way they have organized their movement, by welcoming everyone, eschewing hierarchy, and allowing a voice to whoever shows up, they hope to set an example for the rest of society.

# 11

# The Occupiers Need to Look Past Ideologies to Fight Injustice and Greed

## M. Todd Henderson

*Todd Henderson served as clerk to the Honorable Dennis Jacobs of the US Court of Appeals for the Second Circuit and then practiced appellate litigation at Kirkland & Ellis in Washington, DC. Henderson is now a professor at the University of Chicago Law School. His research interests include corporations, securities regulation, bankruptcy, law and economics, and intellectual property.*

*The slogan "We are the 99 percent" has gained great popularity, but the Occupy Movement is confused about who the elites are in America and who supports their vague goals. Depending on the issue, elites vary greatly, and in terms of social issues, the Occupy Movement does not speak for 99 percent of America. However, social injustices are real, and much can be done to overhaul an unfair financial system. But in order to achieve success, occupiers need to identify their goals and focus on gaining support from a majority of voters.*

The 'Occupy' movement will never succeed against its "one percent" adversaries until it begins to understand that there is not a single one percent, but rather many.

An entire field of economics, known as "public choice," studies how small, concentrated groups with similar interests generally prevail politically against larger groups of diffused interests. And, in our society, these concentrated interests—like unions, defense contractors, religious groups, farmers, etc.—are not necessarily part of the "one percent" Occupy talks about, and several have even joined or co-opted the Movement. But they are part of the broader one-percent problem.

## Defining the 99 Percent

I recently participated in a debate about the Occupy Movement at the university where I teach. The representative from Occupy Chicago claimed to be speaking on behalf of *the* 99 percent, but the problem is that there is no single coherent 99 percent. There are many 99 percents depending on the issue at stake, and any successful 99 percent movement must be more nuanced and draw finer lines than the Occupy Movement has so far.

---

*Even during the height of the recent financial crisis, about 60 percent of Americans still supported capitalism.*

---

When focused broadly on just income or wealth, the message of Occupy is too radical to represent anything close to 99 percent of Americans. The representative of Occupy in the debate identified himself as a Marxist [after Karl Marx's socialist worldview] claimed that the American dream is dead and buried, and argued the only way to solve our problems is for the government to overturn *Citizens United* [Supreme Court decision to grant corporations the same political donation rights as individuals] and dramatically regulate political speech. The problem with this, of course, is that 99 percent of Americans do not support any of these assertions, let alone all of them together.

Even during the height of the recent financial crisis, about 60 percent of Americans still supported capitalism. Most Americans believe the American dream is still alive, and in a 2009 Gallup poll, nearly 60 percent agreed with the Supreme Court that spending on political issues is political speech. At best, about 40 percent of Americans share some of the views of Occupy.

The timing of the Movement is also a bit too convenient to be inclusive of Republicans and Democrats who make up the 99 percent. In 2009, the top one percent took a *smaller* share of national income than in each of the four years of President [Bill] Clinton's second term.

---

*The fact that teachers unions support Occupy undermines its power. A true movement of the 99 percents would be on the side of students, not teachers.*

---

## Allocating Resources

But there is something important about rhetoric of the one percent. "Public choice" economics explores the problems of concentrated interests. There are fewer corn farmers than taxpayers, and the gains from ethanol subsidies are large for each corn farmer, while the costs per taxpayer are quite small. The costs of coordination and the financial incentives mean the farmers will get their way so long as the government has the power to subsidize or penalize. This simple dynamic explains much of how our government allocates resources.

And, unlike Marx or *Citizens United*, it is something the Tea Party and Occupy can agree upon. Although it may seem far-fetched at first glance, if Occupy found common ground with the Tea Party or the sentiments behind it, much could be done politically. After all, there are many 99 percents. But so far, Occupy has absorbed or been co-opted by various one percents.

## Finding Common Ground

For example, in education policy, teachers are the one percent, while students and parents are the 99 percent. But it is generally the power of the concentrated teachers' unions that drives decisions about education spending and policy. The fact that teachers unions support Occupy undermines its power. A true movement of the 99 percents would be on the side of students, not teachers.

Examples abound that cut across typical ideological lines. For instance, military contractors are the one percent, while soldiers and the citizens they defend are the 99 percent. It is for this reason that in the recent census, 7 out of the 10 richest counties surround Washington, D.C.

Although "rich" people are too heterogeneous to be considered a concentrated interest in the same way, this doesn't mean income inequality gets a free pass. For instance, explicit government policies permit very large banks to borrow at significantly lower rates from the federal government than other banks. The about 0.5 percentage point difference translates into hundreds of millions in subsidies, which, according to a recent academic study, is about equal to the excessive compensation earned by the CEOs [chief executive officers] of these banks.

Everyone should be outraged by this policy, regardless of whether you are a fan of Marx or Adam Smith [a pioneer of free markets and capitalism]. And, if Occupy would find these areas of common ground with the rest of the 99 percent of the population, we could start to fight back against all the one percents that distort policies to their favor and against the less powerful.

# 12

# In Order to Succeed, the Occupy Movement Needs to Broaden Its Focus

*Maria Armoudian*

*Maria Armoudian is an author, a fellow at the University of Southern California's Center for International Studies, and the host and producer of the Pacifica Radio programs* The Scholars' Circle *and* The Insighters. *She serves on the board of the Los Angeles League of Conservation Voters and is also a singer/ songwriter.*

*The Occupy movement has already left its mark on politics and changed the public's perception of government and the financial sector. To sustain momentum, the protesters need to employ the media and at the same time launch initiatives to change the political system from within. Previous civil rights movements have taken their battles to the courts and legislatures, and the Occupy Movement might have to follow in their steps to reach their high-minded goals.*

Many supporters of the Occupy demonstrators are agitated over public officials' growing demands that the Occupy settlers move off of the occupied grounds. Might the Occupy movement benefit from moving forward? History teaches us that these moments can catalyze the next wave of a movement, those actions that institutionalize the change that

Maria Armoudian, "How Will the Occupy Movement Evolve?" Truth-Out.org, January 2, 2012. Truth-Out.org. Copyright © 2012 by Maria Armoudian. All rights reserved. Reproduced by permission.

they seek. What might that mean to Occupy? Perhaps it means acknowledging the achievements to date, looking to the lessons of history and assessing what forward means.

---

*Political movements begin with a spark—powerful communications, ideas and demonstrations.*

---

## Striving for Justice

Already, the Occupiers have made an important contribution through their tenacity by their clear articulation about the discrepancy between the American creed and reality, and by their vision for a more just political system. They have taken the first steps toward shaping that vision into reality—declaring the status quo unacceptable—and perhaps now, public officials are forcing the Occupiers' collective hand for their next move in building and developing an effective movement. And here lies the potential of a transformative political movement.

Political movements begin with a spark—powerful communications, ideas and demonstrations. When the spark resonates—as the Occupy movement's has—the movements *can* evolve into a true force of change, much like those historic movements that came before Occupy and delivered true political transformations.

Already, the Occupy movement is groundbreaking in its approach, its breadth and its scope. Among its many contributions, Occupy has made a concise statement about the fundamental incompatibility of many of the elements of the United States' current system with the grand principles that it espouses. It has demanded basic political fairness and equality. It has captured the world's attention and generated new thought about the realities of our political system, broad swathes of empathy and a remarkable solidarity across numerous communities, both in the United States and in the rest of the world.

## Getting the Message Out

Occupiers have generated copious amounts of media coverage—both in their own media and in more traditional outlets. They've branded the all-important phrase, "We are the 99 percent." In the process, they've crowded the shallow, unworkable message of the Tea Party out of the media spotlight. Along with that, they've garnered the ire of those who work hard to preserve the status quo—a system that leaves far too many out in the cold to be considered genuinely democratic.

Simultaneously, many Occupiers have also demonstrated how to build communities with shared values and shared resources such as food, drink, ideas, even libraries. At many Occupy camps, the demonstrators have devised systems of communication and structures that work to hear everyone and diminish no one, from which astute and creative ideas are emerging about how to apply these community values to the country and to the world at large, and how to establish real equality to accompany the ideal one that has been promised but not yet delivered.

---

*Occupiers have generated copious amounts of media coverage—both in their own media and in more traditional outlets. They've branded the all-important phrase, "We are the 99 percent."*

---

Now, at this crossroad, Occupiers are facing at least one important question: What separates successful movements from failed ones? Two of the most successful movements in American history—the civil rights movement and the women's movement—achieved their goals through a multilayered, all-encompassing strategy. Although we most remember their bold, dramatic actions—such as sit-ins, boycotts and Freedom Rides—the vast part of the movement was not quite so conspicuous.

## Changing the System

And these aspects of the movements were what institutionalized the transformations that they sought. These political entrepreneurs were engaged at every level of society, particularly in the halls of power in every level of government. They worked to move laws and policies toward their goals through legislative bodies in cities, counties, states and the Congress. When elected officials hindered their goals toward greater justice and equality, the movement ran their own candidates—and began to win. At the same time, another set of change agents entered federal and state court rooms to challenge the laws and practices that didn't comport with the basic tenets of fairness and equality. They appeared in the Supreme Court to construct civil rights and the meaning of the Constitution.

*Today, there are vast opportunities through multiple media channels to inform, build, challenge, inform and reframe through an increasingly connected world.*

Through it all—the demonstrations and the engagement with the democratic institutions—successful movements established Constitutional amendments, vitally important legislation such as the Civil Rights Act and landmark precedents such as *Brown v. Board of Education* [outlawed segregated schools]. And these laws, precedents and constructions shaped the future of the United States, ultimately making it a more just place.

Of course, none of this would have been possible without winning some battles in the court of public opinion. All political transformations occur on two tracks—on one track, the political entrepreneurs strategically push the transformation forward. On the second track, journalists communicate the change agents' information, ideas and new frameworks to a broader audience.

## New Media Help Political Activism

Historically, such transformations—both in the US and abroad—took decades of challenging the status quo framing of what was or was not acceptable. But the landscape has changed. In the past, political entrepreneurs largely had two choices: first, to pound on the gates to reach the media's gate-keepers, and second, to generate micro-media—fliers and small "mosquito" presses to get their message out. Today, there are vast opportunities through multiple media channels to inform, build, challenge, inform and reframe through an increasingly connected world.

All politics are fluid, dynamic and ever-changing. They ebb and flow because of the interaction between the information, ideas, beliefs, emotions and actions that shape the next moment, and then the next. The Occupiers' next moves are important for both the future of the movement and the future of the law and institutions, which will then shape the future of the United States itself. One possibility is that the official showdown will move the Occupiers from occupying the *lawns* of the institutions to occupying the actual *halls* of the institutions, and perhaps that movement will galvanize the next step in facilitating the realization of its vision. Alternatively, they may return to the lawns, just outside of the wall of power. Or thirdly, they may take both paths, which may be one way to continue moving forward—simultaneously institutionalizing their goals while generating new media based on their successes and failures therein. This is motion, and indeed, the very word, "movement" implies motion.

# 13

# The Occupy Movement Needs Real Leaders and Real Goals

*Akshara Sekar and Deborah Soung*

*Akshara Sekar and Deborah Soung write for the* Saratoga Falcon.

*Unless the Occupy Movement chooses leaders and agrees on common goals, the protests will continue to attract miscreants and hangers-on, who dilute or corrupt the movement's important message. Violence has to be avoided, if protesters hope to achieve their goals of changing society. Only leaders with a grasp of the political process will keep the movement organized.*

There is the oh-so-noble and admirable cause behind the Occupy Wall Street movement to establish a better distribution of economic power in America. Then there are the horror stories: protesters smashing in shop windows and setting barricades ablaze in Oakland, attacking police officers with razor blades, unprovoked in San Francisco, and pushing elderly women down stairs in Washington, D.C.

## The Need for Leaders and Goals

These incidents serve to give the Occupy movement a lawless, anti-authority image, which diverts attention from the movement's true target as well as taint the public perception of the protesters, the majority of whom are peaceful and law-abiding. Until protesters define their purpose in a clear set of goals and accept leaders to represent them, chaos will continue to define their movement and they will be unable to establish the economic equality they are striving for.

---

*As a budding movement with the potential to be enormously influential, much of the American middle class looks to the movement for guidance.*

---

So far, Occupy members have obstinately refused to put down onto paper exactly what they intend to accomplish. Of course, Americans get the gist of their message—that corporations have too much power and that the common people need more money. But until the movement has a concrete destination, they will remain as they are, a stagnant muddle of unhappy citizens standing in front of office buildings.

As a budding movement with the potential to be enormously influential, much of the American middle class looks to the movement for guidance. Therefore, if the movement sets down the goal that corporations should be taxed more, the 99 percent could truly take action. The ordinary citizen could be moved to contact his congressman, which could trigger a bill, and so on.

The reason behind the movement's lack of goals can be attributed to its absence of leaders. Occupy members seem to be allergic to leaders because the protesters believe all leaders have the same goals for self-benefit that allegedly corrupt corporate officials possess.

This fear should not be an excuse. Having a leader does not mean stooping to corruption; having a leader who proves more efficient, effective and trustworthy than the likes of largely disliked corporate officials such as Leo Apotheker, former CEO [chief executive officer] of Hewlett-Packard, means elevating the movement above the level of the mighty One Percent.

## Shedding Violent Hangers-on

The Occupy movement's lack of goals and leaders attract miscreants who misrepresent the movement's true cause. These people think of these protests as an excuse to act violently, and their actions, which often result in bloodshed and violence are wholly unjustified. Unfortunately, just a handful of these criminals in an Occupy demonstration can turn a peaceful protest into a bloody riot, and riots will only serve to tarnish the movement reputation.

Occupy San Diego highlights the dangers of anarchy in the movement. According to CBS Los Angeles, two street vendors were forced to shut down their businesses after protesters smeared blood and urine on their carts. The reason the vendors were attacked reveals the depravity of select protesters: The vendors initially offered free food and drink for protesters during non-business hours, but once they started to charge for their goods again, protesters became angry and began vandalizing their carts.

---

*The Occupy movement should be strengthening the community, not destroying it.*

---

These vendors were trying to show support for the Occupy movement, and they were likely part of the 99 percent the movement claims to represent. The vandalism reveals the dangers of anger without purpose, which will only continue to hinder the movement if protests remain as chaotic as they are now. Occupy members should not be wasting their efforts targeting each other. With a clear goal defined, members will be able to direct their energy toward a better, unified cause against the corporate elite instead of attacking one another.

## Winning over Communities

The Occupy movement should be strengthening the community, not destroying it. With a clearer purpose and real leaders, protests would attract fewer miscreants who show up for the purpose of being able to break the law with a smaller chance of being arrested.

Media coverage on police activity during the protests has been largely unsavory: According to the *New York Observer*, police have allegedly misused pepper spray on protesters and used excessive force when arresting people. The antagonism policemen display toward protesters can likely be attributed to the small number of vandals and criminals in the Occupy movement.

But the only way to convert the population of protesters into a better crowd is to find a leader who can keep local protests organized. Until these riots calm down and the violence stops, local governments are completely justified in attempting to shut down their respective Occupy protests.

# 14

## The Occupy Movement Will Fail

**Human Events**

*Human Events subscribes to the Reaganesque [after former president Ronald Reagan] principles of free enterprise, limited government, and unwavering defense of American freedom and strives to give voice to conservative thinkers.*

*The Occupy Movement is marred by inconsistencies, a lack of agenda and position, and has little chance of convincing the public. Instead of working within law, as was done by the Tea Party, the occupiers revert to violence and attract radicals from the left and right. It poses as a grass-roots movement but is supported and backed by millionaires, celebrities, and liberal democrats.*

The Left was envious when Tea Party protests popped up in 2009, and now has countered with the Occupy Wall Street [OWS] gathering in New York that has spread to other cities. While Tea Party enthusiasm became an effective force during the 2010 elections, OWS will not have the same impact and here is why: The Top 10 Reasons Occupy Wall Street is a joke.

*1. Agenda.* Unlike the clarity of the Tea Party message of smaller government, the Wall Street Occupiers have a potpourri of juvenile demands, from free college education and an annual living wage to "forgiveness of debt on the entire planet." One protester mused that the solution was to do away with money altogether. Apparently these recipients of federal student loans have yet to take Economics 101.

*2. Celebrities.* The usual suspects of empty-headed progressive Hollywood stars are showing up at the Wall Street rally, many arriving by limo. Millionaires Tim Robbins, Susan Sarandon, Michael Moore and Roseanne Barr have all made appearances. Kanye West wore gold jewelry worth more than many protesters have made in their lifetimes. If they hadn't noticed, these stars are part of the 1%.

*3. Soros.* The roster of George Soros [business magnate and philanthropist]-funded entities are aiding and abetting the Occupy movement. *AdBusters*, an anti-consumerist publication that sounded the initial call for the protests, is funded in part by Tides, a major recipient of Soros' funding. Another Soros venture—*MoveOn.org*—has rallied support for the initiative. Soros, a billionaire several times over largely through currency manipulation, says he "sympathizes with their grievances" of those protesting corporate greed.

---

*Kanye West wore gold jewelry [to a rally] worth more than many protesters have made in their lifetimes.*

---

*4. Arrests.* Unlike the Tea Party rallies, there have been numerous arrests at the Occupy protests, as the crowds ignore city ordinances about overnight camping on public property. Nearly a thousand were arrested in New York for blocking the Brooklyn Bridge, snarling traffic for those who work for a living, and hundreds have been taken into custody in Chicago, Boston and other cities.

*5. Politics.* Democrats from President [Barack] Obama on down are trying to find common ground with the Occupy Wall Streeters, hoping the protests can be the liberal equivalent of the Tea Party and breathe some life into a moribund progressive movement. The hypocrisy is riper—the President has garnered more corporate donations than any politician in the nation's history.

*6. Unpatriotic.* OWS protests routinely view the United States as the enemy. The American flag is trashed, desecrated and flown upside down. A Coast Guard female officer in uniform was harassed and spit on near the Boston rally. In Portland, Ore., a speaker said, "F**k America." The protesters would like nothing better than to see the decline of their country.

*7. Extremists.* It is no small feat to be praised by both the American Nazi Party and the Communist Party USA. From aging hippies who are trying to relive the glory of the Sixties to the younger anarchists who have nothing better to do, many of the OWS protesters are extremists who show up at every left-wing demonstration.

*8. Trash.* After Tea Party rallies, the grounds were generally swept clean of garbage by the protesters, leaving the areas cleaner than before they arrived. In contrast, at OWS protests, piles of trash are mounting, creating a public health hazard. And after several weeks, many in the crowd are in dire need of a shower.

*9. Anti-Semitic.* While the mainstream media pushed a fictitious story line that the Tea Party was a cauldron of racism, the OWS rallies feature plenty of examples of outright anti-Semitism. The rallies are marrying the anti-Zionist tirades of the Left with the stereotypical view of Jewish Wall Street bankers to create an ugly atmosphere.

*10. Signs.* The Tea Party rallies were always full of clever signs, poking fun at Big Government and Barack Obama, and honoring the Founding Fathers and the Constitution. By contrast, the Occupy Wall Street signs are characterized by misspelled words, profanity and inane statements such as, "One day the poor will have nothing left to eat but the rich."

# 15

# The Occupy Movement Is a Peaceful Protest

*Rebecca Solnit*

*Rebecca Solnit is an activist and the author of many books, in-cluding* Wanderlust: A History of Walking, The Battle of The Story of the Battle in Seattle, Storming The Gates of Paradise: Landscapes for Politics, *and* A Paradise Built in Hell. *She is a contributing editor for* Harper's Magazine.

*The Occupy Movement is entering a critical phase in early 2012. The honeymoon is over, and if the movement wants to survive, it has to overcome police brutality as well as vandals that have infiltrated their ranks. Furthermore, occupiers need to overcome biased media coverage, which often sides with politicians and police who try to discredit the protesters and paint a distorted picture of the non-violent protests. The political landscape has started to transform, but the Occupy Movement can become an agent of lasting change only if it can keep the debate about the future of American society alive by pressuring legislatures and courts alike.*

When you fall in love, it's all about what you have in common, and you can hardly imagine that there are differences, let alone that you will quarrel over them, or weep about them, or be torn apart by them—or if all goes well, struggle, learn, and bond more strongly because of, rather than despite, them. The Occupy movement had its glorious honeymoon when old and young, liberal and radical, comfortable and desperate, homeless and tenured all found that what they had in common was so compelling the differences hardly seemed to matter.

Until they did.

Revolutions are always like this: at first all men are brothers and anything is possible, and then, if you're lucky, the romance of that heady moment ripens into a relationship, instead of a breakup, an abusive marriage, or a murder-suicide. Occupy had its golden age, when those who never before imagined living side-by-side with homeless people found themselves in adjoining tents in public squares.

---

*Occupy had its golden age, when those who never before imagined living side-by-side with homeless people found themselves in adjoining tents in public squares.*

---

## Fighting Greed and Privatization

All sorts of other equalizing forces were present, not least the police brutality that battered the privileged the way that inner-city kids are used to being battered all the time. Part of what we had in common was what we were against: the current economy and the principle of insatiable greed that made it run, as well as the emotional and economic privatization that accompanied it.

This is a system that damages people, and its devastation was on display as never before in the early months of Occupy and related phenomena like the *We are the 99%* website. When it was people facing foreclosure, or who'd lost their jobs, or were thrashing around under avalanches of college or medical debt, they weren't hard to accept as *us*, and not *them*.

And then came the people who'd been damaged far more, the psychologically fragile, the marginal, and the homeless— some of them endlessly needy and with a huge capacity for disruption. People who had come to fight the power found themselves staying on to figure out available mental-health resources, while others who had wanted to experience a democratic society on a grand scale found themselves trying to solve sanitation problems.

And then there was the violence.

---

*It has been a sustained campaign of police brutality from Wall Street to Washington State the likes of which we haven't seen in 40 years.*

---

## The Faces of Violence

The most important direct violence Occupy faced was, of course, from the state, in the form of the police using maximum sub-lethal force on sleepers in tents, mothers with children, unarmed pedestrians, young women already penned up, unresisting seated students, poets, professors, pregnant women, wheelchair-bound occupiers, and octogenarians [people in their eighties]. It has been a sustained campaign of police brutality from Wall Street to Washington State the likes of which we haven't seen in 40 years.

On the part of activists, there were also a few notable incidents of violence in the hundreds of camps, especially violence against women. The mainstream media seemed to think this damned the Occupy movement, though it made the camps, at worst, a whole lot like the rest of the planet, which, in case you hadn't noticed, seethes with violence against women. But these were isolated incidents.

## Reclaiming the World

That old line of songster Woody Guthrie is always handy in situations like this: "Some will rob you with a six-gun, some with a fountain pen." The police have been going after occupiers with projectile weapons, clubs, and tear gas, sending some of them to the hospital and leaving more than a few others traumatized and fearful. That's the six-gun here.

But it all began with the fountain pens, slashing through peoples' lives, through national and international economies, through the global markets. These were wielded by the banksters, the "vampire squid," the deregulators in D.C., the men—and with the rarest of exceptions they were men—who stole the world.

That's what Occupy came together to oppose, the grandest violence by scale, the least obvious by impact. No one on Wall Street ever had to get his suit besmirched by carrying out a foreclosure eviction himself. Cities provided that service for free to the banks (thereby further impoverishing themselves as they created new paupers out of old taxpayers). And the police clubbed their opponents for them, over and over, everywhere across the United States.

The grand thieves invented ever more ingenious methods, including those sliced and diced derivatives, to crush the hopes and livelihoods of the many. This is the terrible violence that Occupy was formed to oppose. Don't ever lose sight of that.

## Oakland's Nonviolence

Now that we're done remembering the major violence, let's talk about Occupy Oakland [California]. A great deal of fuss has been made about two incidents in which mostly young people affiliated with Occupy Oakland damaged some property and raised some hell.

The mainstream media and some faraway pundits weighed in on those Bay Area incidents as though they determined the meaning and future of the transnational Occupy phenomenon. Perhaps some of them even hoped, consciously or otherwise, that harped on enough these might divide or destroy the movement. So it's important to recall that the initial impact of Occupy Oakland was the very opposite of violent, stunningly so, in ways that were intentionally suppressed.

Occupy Oakland began in early October [2011] as a vibrant, multiracial gathering. A camp was built at Oscar Grant/ Frank Ogawa Plaza, and thousands received much-needed meals and healthcare for free from well-organized volunteers. Sometimes called the Oakland Commune, it was consciously descended from some of the finer aspects of an earlier movement born in Oakland, the Black Panthers, whose free breakfast programs should perhaps be as well-remembered and more admired than their macho posturing.

---

*This country is segregated in so many terrible ways— and then it wasn't for those glorious weeks when civil society awoke and fell in love with itself.*

---

A compelling and generous-spirited General Assembly took place nightly and then biweekly in which the most important things on Earth were discussed by wildly different participants. Once, for instance, I was in a breakout discussion group that included Native American, white, Latino, and able-bodied and disabled Occupiers, and in which I was likely the eldest participant; another time, a bunch of peacenik grandmothers dominated my group.

## Bridging the Divide

This country is segregated in so many terrible ways—and then it wasn't for those glorious weeks when civil society awoke and fell in love with itself. Everyone showed up; everyone talked to everyone else; and in little tastes, in fleeting moments, the old divides no longer divided us and we felt like we could imagine ourselves as one society. This was the dream of the promised land—this land, that is, without its bitter divides. Honey never tasted sweeter, and power never felt better.

Now here's something astonishing. While the camp was in existence, crime went down 19% in Oakland, a statistic the city was careful to conceal. "It may be counter to our statement that the Occupy movement is negatively impacting crime in Oakland," the police chief wrote to the mayor in an email that local news station KTVU later obtained and released to little fanfare. Pay attention: Occupy was so powerful a force for nonviolence that it was already solving Oakland's chronic crime and violence problems just by giving people hope and meals and solidarity and conversation.

The police attacking the camp knew what the rest of us didn't: Occupy was abating crime, including violent crime, in this gritty, crime-ridden city. "You gotta give them hope," said an elected official across the bay once upon a time—a city supervisor named Harvey Milk. Occupy was hope we gave ourselves, the dream come true. The city did its best to take the hope away violently at 5 a.m. on October 25th [2011]. The sleepers were assaulted; their belongings confiscated and trashed. Then, Occupy Oakland rose again. Many thousands of nonviolent marchers shut down the Port of Oakland in a stunning display of popular power on November 2nd.

## Violence Can Hurt the Movement

That night, some kids did the smashy-smashy stuff that everyone gets really excited about. (They even spray-painted "smashy" on a Rite Aid drugstore in giant letters.) When we talk about people who spray-paint and break windows and start bonfires in the street and shove people and scream and run around, making a demonstration into something way too much like the punk rock shows of my youth, let's keep one thing in mind: they didn't send anyone to the hospital, drive any seniors from their homes, spread despair and debt among the young, snatch food and medicine from the desperate, or destroy the global economy.

That said, they are still a problem. They are the bait the police take and the media go to town with. They create a situation a whole lot of us don't like and that drives away many who might otherwise participate or sympathize. They are, that is, incredibly bad for a movement, and represent a form of segregation by intimidation.

But don't confuse the pro-vandalism Occupiers with the vampire squid or the up-armored robocops who have gone after us almost everywhere. Though their means are deeply flawed, their ends are not so different than yours. There's no question that they should improve their tactics or maybe just act tactically, let alone strategically, and there's no question that a lot of other people should stop being so apocalyptic about it.

Those who advocate for nonviolence at Occupy should remember that nonviolence is at best a great spirit of love and generosity, not a prissy enforcement squad. After all, the Reverend Martin Luther King, Jr., who gets invoked all the time when such issues come up, didn't go around saying grumpy things about Malcolm X and the Black Panthers.

---

*[D]on't confuse the pro-vandalism Occupiers with the vampire squid or the up-armored robocops who have gone after us almost everywhere.*

---

## Violence Against the Truth

Of course, a lot of people responding to these incidents in Oakland are actually responding to fictional versions of them. In such cases, you could even say that some journalists were doing violence against the truth of what happened in Oakland on November 2nd [2011] and January 28th [2012].

The *San Francisco Chronicle*, for example, reported on the day's events this way:

"Among the most violent incidents that occurred Saturday night was in front of the YMCA at 23rd Street and Broadway. Police corralled protesters in front of the building and several dozen protesters stormed into the Y, apparently to escape from the police, city officials and protesters said. Protesters damaged a door and a few fixtures, and frightened those inside the gym working out, said Robert Wilkins, president of the YMCA of the East Bay."

Wilkins was apparently not in the building, and first-person testimony recounts that a YMCA staff member welcomed the surrounded and battered protesters, and once inside, some were so terrified they pretended to work out on exercise machines to blend in.

I wrote this to the journalists who described the incident so peculiarly: "What was violent about [activists] fleeing police engaging in wholesale arrests and aggressive behavior? Even the YMCA official who complains about it adds, 'The damage appears pretty minimal.' And you call it violence? That's sloppy."

The reporter who responded apologized for what she called her "poor word choice" and said the piece was meant to convey police violence as well.

## Police Violence Goes Unnoticed and Unpunished

When the police are violent against activists, journalists tend to frame it as though there were violence in some vaguely unascribable sense that implicates the clobbered as well as the clobberers. In, for example, the build-up to the 2004 Republican National Convention in New York City, the mainstream media kept portraying the right of the people peaceably to assemble as tantamount to terrorism and describing all the terrible things that the government or the media themselves speculated we might want to do (but never did).

Some of this was based on the fiction of tremendous activist violence in Seattle in 1999 that the *New York Times* in particular devoted itself to promulgating. That the police smashed up nonviolent demonstrators and constitutional rights pretty badly in both Seattle and New York didn't excite them nearly as much. Don't forget that before the obsession with violence arose, the smearing of Occupy was focused on the idea that people weren't washing very much, and before that the framework for marginalization was that Occupy had "no demands." There's always something.

Keep in mind as well that Oakland's police department is on the brink of federal receivership for not having made real amends for old and well-documented problems of violence, corruption, and mismanagement, and that it was the police department, not the Occupy Oakland demonstrators, which used tear gas, clubs, smoke grenades, and rubber bullets on January 28th. It's true that a small group vandalized City Hall after the considerable police violence, but that's hardly what the plans were at the outset of the day.

The action on January 28th that resulted in 400 arrests and a media conflagration was called Move-In Day. There was a handmade patchwork banner that proclaimed "Another Oakland Is Possible" and a children's contingent with pennants, balloons, and strollers. Occupy Oakland was seeking to take over an abandoned building so that it could reestablish the community, the food programs, and the medical clinic it had set up last fall. It may not have been well planned or well executed, but it was idealistic.

Despite this, many people who had no firsthand contact with Occupy Oakland inveighed against it or even against the whole Occupy movement. If only that intensity of fury were to be directed at the root cause of it all, the colossal economic violence that surrounds us.

All of which is to say, for anyone who hadn't noticed, that the honeymoon is over.

## The Real Work

The honeymoon is, of course, the period when you're so in love you don't notice differences that will eventually have to be worked out one way or another. Most relationships begin as though you were coasting downhill. Then come the flat-lands, followed by the hills where you're going to have to pedal hard, if you don't just abandon the bike.

Occupy might just be the name we've put on a great groundswell of popular outrage and a rebirth of civil society too deep, too broad, to be a movement. A movement is an ocean wave: this is the whole tide turning from Cairo to Moscow to Athens to Santiago to Chicago. Nevertheless, the American swell in this tide involves a delicate alliance between liberals and radicals, people who want to reform the government and campaign for particular gains, and people who wish the government didn't exist and mostly want to work outside the system. If the radicals should frighten the liberals as little as possible, surely the liberals have an equal obligation to get fiercer and more willing to confront—and to remember that nonviolence, even in its purest form, is not the same as being nice.

Surely the only possible answer to the tired question of where Occupy should go from here (as though a few public figures got to decide) is: everywhere. I keep being asked what Occupy should do next, but it's already doing it. It *is* everywhere.

---

*Occupy might just be the name we've put on a great groundswell of popular outrage and a rebirth of civil society too deep, too broad, to be a movement.*

---

In many cities, outside the limelight, people are still occupying public space in tents and holding General Assemblies. February 20th [2012], for instance, was a national day of Occupy solidarity with prisoners; Occupiers are organizing on many fronts and planning for May Day, and a great many foreclosure defenses from Nashville to San Francisco have kept people in their homes and made banks renegotiate. Campus activism is reinvigorated, and creative and fierce discussions about college costs and student debt are underway, as is a deeper conversation about economics and ethics that rejects conventional wisdom about what is fair and possible.

## Gaining Ground and Support

Occupy is one catalyst or facet of the populist will you can see in a host of recent victories. The campaign against corporate personhood seems to be gaining momentum. A popular environmental campaign made President [Barack] Obama reject the Keystone XL tar sands pipeline from Canada, despite immense Republican and corporate pressure. In response to widespread outrage, the Susan B. Komen Foundation reversed its decision to defund cancer detection at Planned Parenthood. Online campaigns have forced Apple to address its hideous labor issues, and the ever-heroic Coalition of Immokalee Workers at last brought Trader Joe's into line with its fair wages for farmworkers campaign.

These genuine gains come thanks to relatively modest exercises of popular power. They should act as reminders that we do have power and that its exercise can be popular. Some of last fall's exhilarating conversations have faltered, but the great conversation that is civil society awake and arisen hasn't stopped.

What happens now depends on vigorous participation, including yours, in thinking aloud together about who we are, what we want, and how we get there, and then acting upon it. Go occupy the possibilities and don't stop pedaling. And remember, it started with mad, passionate love.

# 16

# The Occupy Movement Is Turning Violent

*Megan McArdle*

*Megan McArdle is a senior editor for* The Atlantic, *where she writes about business and economics. She has worked at three start-ups, a consulting firm, an investment bank, a disaster recovery firm at Ground Zero, and* The Economist.

*While Occupy protesters in Oakland were unfairly attacked by the Oakland police, the growing hostility among participants is eroding goodwill toward the movement. Publicity stunts appear to verge on bullying and brutality and undermine the message of the protesters. If the Occupy Movement does not want to lose public support and the chance of changing the political landscape, it needs to crack down on those who destroy it from within.*

Cards on the table: y'all know that the Occupy protests and I don't agree politically. Nonetheless, I've been basically supportive of their right to protest, sympathetic to their frustrations with the system, and interested in their problems (and solutions) of self organization in a rather chaotic and fluid situation. Unless there were clear and dramatic harms to the community, I figured the cops should leave them alone until the protests dispersed naturally.

## Losing the Moral High Ground

I thought the Oakland police overreached in clearing out the park, and overreached when protesters tried to retake it. But while I have ongoing questions about the behavior of the police, the Oakland protesters are rapidly losing whatever moral high ground they gained during that confrontation. The correct response to overly enthusiastic crowd control is not "using homemade bomb launchers to fire M80s at the police" who are trying to stop you from blockading the port, seizing city-owned buildings, and setting fire to things in the downtown Oakland area. Some of the protesters in Oakland seem to think that a wounded veteran somehow gives them moral and political license to engage in . . . well, it's getting perilously close to the point where the correct word is indisputably "rioting".

---

*Muttering "There oughta be a law" doesn't count.*

---

Then there's the group of 500 people who surrounded Jamie Dimon's [CEO of JP Morgan Chase & Co] hotel in Seattle and promised to make a citizen's arrest. I assume they were looking for a stunt, not trying to invoke echoes of a lynch mob—but citizen's arrest is for people who have been caught in the commission of a clear violation of the law. Muttering "There oughta be a law" doesn't count. And having a large, angry group gather for the proclaimed purpose of taking a single person into physical custody is creepy—yes, even if it's impractical. Plus, it affords obvious opportunities for something to go spectacularly, catastrophically wrong.

As I said to the tea partiers who carried guns to protests: this sort of thing should stop. Not because you don't have a right to it, but because it frightens people. And large political protests should strive to avoid things that make others afraid for their physical safety, even if you know in your heart that you mean no harm. Whoever organized this should have known better.

## Staying Within the Law

Remember all the paranoia about the "violent undertone" at tea party protests? Some of the things happening at a few of these protests is starting to seem like more than an undertone. I would far rather have my neighbor stand outside his house with a gun, than have him lob fireworks at my house, or get a bunch of his friends to cordon off my house so they could "arrest me." The tea party [movement] were demonstrating in a combined space and making life a little hot for legislators. These people are roaming around in mobs, damaging property and repeatedly clashing with the police. And no, I'm afraid I don't think that this is because the police are biased against left wing protesters; I think it's because the tea partiers stayed within the law.

---

*Camping in a public park is a harmless extension of one's public rights. Barricading ports, shutting down streets, breaking into buildings, and setting bonfires . . . these are not.*

---

## Losing Public Support

Perhaps I am overreacting, but the events in Oakland seem to suggest that some faction of that group, at least, is not trying to work change within the system; they're trying to take over bits of it by force. Camping in a public park is a harmless extension of one's public rights. Barricading ports, shutting down streets, breaking into buildings, and setting bonfires . . . these are not.

I think that goes too far for most people. It certainly does for me. And the latest poll from Quinnipiac seems to indicate that the growing public disorder is costing them the high levels of support they once enjoyed. A few weeks ago, a *Time* poll showed that Occupy Wall Street [OWS] had about twice as much public support as the tea party. Now their unfavorables are higher than their favorables, and both are only a few points better than the tea partiers. Among independents, they're indistinguishable.

And that poll was taken before things got really out of hand in Oakland. How will those numbers look a few days from now?

I don't want to minimize the things that have been done to protesters—I think the police should have exercised far more restraint, and if it's true that a man deliberately ran his car into jaywalking protesters yesterday, he deserves to be in jail. But that's not an excuse for rioting.

At this point, the movement is hurting itself more than it's helping—at least, if you think their goal is to peacefully and democratically push for changes in the laws, a task for which they are going to require some support beyond the committed left. If you don't, of course . . . well, that has all sorts of implications.

If I suggest that the movement, and the left, needs to control this before the public really turns on OWS, I'll be accused of concern trolling. So I'll just say that despite our substantial disagreements, (and doubts about the effectiveness) I've been broadly supportive of the OWS project of organizing for change. However, if events continue to go in an Oakland direction, I'm going to become rather hostile to the movement. And I doubt that I'm the only one.

# Organizations to Contact

*The editors have compiled the following list of organizations concerned with the issues debated in this book. The descriptions are derived from materials provided by the organizations. All have publications or information available for interested readers. The list was compiled on the date of publication of the present volume; the information provided here may change. Be aware that many organizations take several weeks or longer to respond to inquiries, so allow as much time as possible.*

## InterOccupy

e-mail: info@occupytogether.org
website: www.interoccupy.org

InterOccupy seeks to foster communication between individuals, Working Groups, and local General Assemblies across the Occupy movement, using direct democratic and horizontal decision-making processes. InterOccupy hosts conference calls using Maestro conference call technology, which allows up to 500 people to interact productively on phones. Statements and articles about the Occupy Movement's activities as well as scheduled talks and events are available on the InterOccupy website.

## National Lawyers Guild (NLG)

132 Nassau Street, #922, New York, NY   10038
website: www.nlg.org/occupy/

The National Lawyers Guild (NLG) is dedicated to changing the structure of our political and economic system. It seeks to unite American lawyers, law students, legal workers, and jailhouse lawyers to build an effective political and social force in the service of the people. The organization believes that human rights are more important than property interests. The Guild has been conducting mass defense for over half a century. Books and other publications can be accessed or purchased on NLG's website.

## National People's Action (NPA)

810 N. Milwaukee, Chicago, IL 60642
(312) 243-3035
website: www.npa-us.org

National People's Action (NPA) is a network of grassroots organizations that works to advance a national economic and racial justice agenda. NPA has over 200 organizers working to unite everyday people in cities, towns, and rural communities throughout the United States via direct-action, house meetings, and community organizing. Materials on the Occupy Movement and other grassroots organizations are available at the NPA website.

## New York Communities for Change

2-4 Nevins St, 2nd Fl., Brooklyn, NY 11217
(347) 410-6919
e-mail: info@nycommunities.org
website: www.nycommunities.org

New York Communities for Change is a coalition of working families in low and moderate income communities who are fighting for social and economic justice throughout New York State. By using direct action, legislative advocacy, and community organizing, NY Communities' members work to influence the political and economic policies that directly affect them.

## Occupy Our Homes

website: http://occupyourhomes.org

Occupy Our Homes believes that everyone deserves to have a roof over their head and a place to call home. According to Occupy Our Homes, having a decent place to live is the most fundamental part of the American dream, a source of security and pride. Occupy Our Homes supports Americans whose homes are under threat of foreclosure. Videos such as *How to Defend Your Home* are available on the organization's website.

## Occupy Wall Street (OWS)

The UPS Store, Re: Occupy Wall Street
New York, NY 10038
(516) 708-4777

e-mail: general@occupywallst.org
website: http://occupywallst.org

OccupyWallSt.org is the unofficial *de facto* online resource for the occupation movement that began on Wall Street. They are an affinity group committed to providing technical support work for resistance movements; public discussion boards and livestreams are provided on their website.

### Occupied Wall Street Journal
e-mail: occupymedia@gmail.com
website: http://occupiedmedia.us/

The *Occupied Wall Street Journal,* an OWS affinity group, is a media project participating in the Occupy movement. Run entirely by volunteers, the *Occupied Wall Street Journal* operates on the basis of donations.

### Unitarian Universalist Service Committee (UUSC)
689 Massachusetts Avenue, Cambridge, MA   02139-3302
(617) 868-6600
website: http://actnow.uusc.org

The Unitarian Universalist Service Committee (UUSC) is a nonsectarian organization that seeks to advance human rights and social justice in the United States and around the world. Through a combination of advocacy, education, and partnerships with grassroots organizations, UUSC promotes economic rights, advances environmental justice, defends civil liberties, and preserves the rights of people in times of humanitarian crisis. The UUSC has joined the Occupy Movement in decrying the wealth disparity that leaves millions struggling for economic security. Publications such as the *Rights Now* newsletter are available UUSC website.

# Bibliography

## Books

| | |
|---|---|
| Adam Cornelius Bert | *Occupy Movement*. Mauritius: Chromo Publishing, 2012. |
| Carla Blumenkranz, Keith Gessen, Mark Greif, and Sarah Leonard | *Occupy!: Scenes from Occupied America*. New York: Verso, 2011. |
| Janet Byrne | *The Occupy Handbook*. Boston, MA: Back Bay Books, 2012. |
| Gwendolyn Chen | *Occupy Wall Street: Social Networks and The Arab Spring*. London, UK: Pearce Heart Group, 2011. |
| Lenny Flank | *Voices from the 99 Percent: An Oral History of the Occupy Wall Street Movement*. St. Petersburg, FL: Red and Black Publishers, 2011. |
| Michael Kazin | *American Dreamers: How the Left Changed a Nation*. New York: Knopf, 2011. |
| Amy Lang and Daniel Lang/Levitsky | *Dreaming in Public: Creating the Occupy Movement*. Toronto, Canada: World Changing, 2012. |
| Kalle Lasn and Adbusters | *Occupy 101: The Creative Destruction of Neoclassical Economics*. New York: Seven Stories Press, 2012. |

Lynn Parramore, Tara Lohan, and Don Hazen — *The 99%: How the Occupy Wall Street Movement Is Changing America.* Alternet, 2011.

J. T. Ross Jackson — *Occupy World Street: A Global Roadmap for Radical Economic and Political Reform.* White River Junction, VT: Chelsea Green Publishing, 2012.

Clay Shirky — *Here Comes Everybody, The Power of Organisation with Organisations.* London: Penguin Press, 2008.

*Time* — *What Is Occupy?: Inside the Global Movement.* New York: Time, 2011.

Sarah van Gelder and Staff of YES! Magazine — *This Changes Everything: Occupy Wall Street and the 99% Movement.* San Francisco: Berrett-Koehler Publishers, 2011.

Richard Wolff and David Barsamian — *Occupy the Economy: Challenging Capitalism.* San Francisco: City Lights Publishers, 2012.

## Periodicals and Internet Sources:

Ben Baden — "15 Stunning Statistics About the Jobs Market," *US News & World Report*, September 28, 2011.

Joseph Berger — "Cries of Anti-Semitism, but Not at Zuccotti Park," *The New York Times*, October 21, 2011.

Ben Berkowitz — "From a Single Hashtag, a Protest Circled the World," *Brisbane Times*, October 19, 2011.

| | |
|---|---|
| Shannon Bond | "Occupy Sets Its Sights Beyond Wall Street," *Financial Times*, December 7, 2011. |
| Tina Dupuy | "The Occupy Movement's Woman Problem," *The Atlantic*, Nov. 21, 2011. |
| *Esquire* | "The Great Occupation," January 2012. |
| Andrew Fleming | "Adbusters Sparks Wall Street Protest Vancouver-based Activists Behind Street Actions in the US," *The Vancouver Courier*, September 27, 2011. |
| Adam Gabbatt | "Occupy Oakland: Demonstrators Prepare for Police Action - Monday 11," *The Guardian*, November 14, 2011. |
| Gloria Goodale | "Weekend Violence in Oakland: Is Occupy Movement Back, or Broken?," *The Christian Science Monitor*, January 30, 2012. |
| David Graeber | "Occupy and Anarchism's Gift of Democracy," *The Guardian*, 15 November, 2011. |
| Steven Greenhouse | "Occupy Movement Inspires Unions to Embrace Bold Tactics," *New York Times*, November 8, 2011. |

Aran Gupta "What Occupy Taught the Unions: SEIU and Others are Embracing the Movement That Has Succeeded as They Have Failed," *Salon*, February 2, 2012.

Elizabeth Harris "Citing Police Trap, Protesters File Suit," *New York Times*, October 5, 2011.

Laird Harrison "Occupy Movement Split over Confrontational Tactics," *Reuters*, February 1, 2012.

Colleen Jenkins and Cynthia Johnston "New York Police Arrest Dozens of Anti-Wall Street Protesters," *Reuters*, January 1, 2012.

Naomi Klein "Occupy Wall Street: The Most Important Thing in the World Now," *The Nation*, October 6, 2011.

Gordon Lafer "What 'Right to Work' Means for Indiana's Workers: A Pay Cut," *The Nation*, January 11, 2012.

Laura Marcinek "Wall Street Areas Blocked as Police Arrest Seven in Protest," *Bloomsberg Businessweek*, September 19, 2011.

Colin Moynihan "80 Arrested as Financial District Protest Moves North," *New York Times*, September 2011.

Mattathias Schwartz "Pre-Occupied. The Origins and Future of Occupy Wall Street," *The New Yorker*, December 29, 2011.

Kim Scipes            "Open Letter to the Occupy Wall
                      Street Movement: Beware of Labor
                      Leaders Bearing Gifts," *Z Net*,
                      October 12, 2011.

Clay Shirky           "The Political Power of Social
                      Media," *Foreign Affairs*, January 2011.

Linda Solomon         "Adbusters' Kalle Lasn: The Flawed
                      Genius Behind Occupy Wall Street,"
                      *Vancouver Observer*, October 12,
                      2011.

Peter Walker          "Occupy London Sets out Agenda on
                      How It Wants to Change the
                      Economic World," *The Guardian*,
                      November 28, 2011.

# Index

University of California Berkeley, 36, 46, 47
US Department of State, 37–38

# V

*V for Vendetta* (film), 40
Vandalism. *See* Crime, as protest action; Crime, protest sites
Veterans, protests, 42, 65, 106
"Vibe" (app), 75
Video documentation and sharing, 36, 46, 75
"Viola" (literary character), 8
Violence. *See* Crime, as protest action; Crime, protest sites; Peace; Police brutality; Violence against women
Violence against women, 96
Viral media content, 36, 46, 75
Volcker Rule (Dodd-Frank Wall Street Reform and Consumer Protection Act, 2010), 74
Voting rights movements, 27–28

# W

Walker, Birgitte, 74
Wall Street. *See* Occupy Wall Street
Walton, Sam, 16
Wars
    literature inspiration, 7
    U.S imperialism, 67, 68
Washington, D.C., 24, 25, 26, 27, 76, 81
Wealth inequality, US
    caused by capital inequality, 21–22
    history, and causes, 55–56

Occupy movement is misled, 15–18, 19, 21
Occupy movement protest core, 10, 11, 24–29, 32, 36, 39–40, 48, 59, 64, 83, 95–96
political solutions, brainstorming, 8–9
visual representations, 15–16
*See also* The 99%; The 1%; Power inequality, systemic
Wealth totals, US
    historic growth, 16–17
    unlimited, 16, 33–34
Wences, Bonnie, 52–53
Whistleblowers, 45
WikiLeaks, 35, 37–38, 40, 44–46
Wilkins, Robert, 101
Winfrey, Oprah, 17
"Within the system" change
    calls for continued, 11–12, 94, 103–104, 108
    civil rights movement and Occupy movement, 45, 82, 85–86, 88
    Tea Party, 91, 107
Women's movement, 12, 84
Women's suffrage, 27–28
Woolworth's lunch counter protests (1960), 51
World Trade Organization protests, Seattle (1999), 28, 37, 38, 41, 51, 101–102
World War II, 12

# Y

YouTube, 75

# Z

Zeese, Kevin, 24–29

CPSIA information can be obtained
at www.ICGtesting.com
Printed in the USA
FFOW020535271112
341FF

9 780737 764871

**Sidney Silverman Library**
**and Learning Resource Center**
**Bergen Community College**
**400 Paramus Road**
**Paramus, NJ 07652-1595**

www.bergen.edu
Return Postage Guaranteed